Great Year-Round

GRILLING
in the
SOUTHEAST

The Flavors • The Culinary Traditions • The Techniques

Ellen Brown

The Lyons Press
Guilford, Connecticut
An Imprint of the Globe Pequot Press

The Lyons Press is an imprint of The Globe Pequot Press.

Photos on the following pages courtesy of Shutterstock: x, 3, 7, 9, 12, 14, 16, 18, 21, 30, 35, 38, 39, 45, 47, 51, 59, 62, 64, 67, 72, 77, 80, 82, 89, 91, 94, 96, 98, 106, 107, 108, 122, 125

Photos on the following pages courtesy of Jupiterimages: 1, 2, 5, 25, 27, 33, 54, 56, 70, 100, 102, 104, 113, 116, 120

Photos on page ix courtesy of the Library of Congress
Text design by Sheryl P. Kober

Library of Congress Cataloging-in-Publication Data

Brown, Ellen.
 Great year-round grilling in the Southeast : the flavors--the culinary traditions--the techniques / Ellen Brown.
   p. cm.
 ISBN 978-1-59921-484-9
 1. Barbecue cookery--Southern States. 2. Cookery, American--Southern style. I. Title.
 TX840.B3B75786 2009
 641.7'60975--dc22

                    2008042714

Printed in China

10 9 8 7 6 5 4 3 2 1

This book is dedicated to Nancy and Walter Dubler, my beloved sister and brother-in-law, with my eternal thanks for all your support.

Contents

This chapter includes everything you need to know about grills and grilling to successfully cook all the recipes in the book, beginning with the principles of grilling; charcoal vs. gas grills; accessories for ease and safety; grilling safety; how to gauge when the grill is ready to cook; how to use wood chips to add smoky flavor to foods; and how to create multi-level fires.

There are four basic ways to flavor food before it goes on the grill—rubs, pastes, marinades, and brines—and the amount of time required to impart flavor ranges from seconds to days. Some include flavors from the Southern and Gulf Coast states, and others encompass other regions of American cooking as well as cuisines from around the world.

This chapter includes sauces to dress up grilled food and elevate a simple entree to a dish of distinction. These sauces are versatile, and can go with many types of food; each recipe is annotated with the categories of grilled food for which it is compatible.

Grilled hors d'oeuvres are as varied as slices of toasted bruschetta topped with fresh tomatoes to Thai chicken satay with peanut sauce. What differentiates hors d'oeuvres from appetizers is that the former are "finger food" and can be eaten without a plate and fork.

From the corn in Grilled Corn Soup to the eggplants, squash, and peppers in Farmer's market Vegetable Soup, grilling adds its flavor to the main ingredients that go into soups, and in the same way small salads can be topped with grilled fare or include grilled ingredients. The salads in this chapter are small appetizers rather than the larger entree salads of Chapter 11.

Contents

Chapter 6: **Fish and Seafood** 38
This region is rich with aquatic species from the Gulf of Mexico as well as warm waters of the southern Atlantic Ocean. The recipes in this chapter highlight shrimp and Gulf Coast species such as red snapper, as well as fish caught in waters around the world.

Chapter 7: **Poultry** 45
Grilled chicken is popular in every region of this country and around the world. The recipes in this chapter encompass cuisines from many continents, and utilize whole birds, mixed parts, and quick-grilling boneless, skinless breasts. The poultry world includes more feathered friends than chicken, so this chapter also includes recipes for turkey and duck, and it begins with a section on how prepare chicken so it cooks best on the grill.

Chapter 8: **Beef and Venison** 52
Grilling steaks on the grill is part and parcel of life if you list yourself among the ranks of carnivores. Even on a gas grill, the aroma and flavor of a grilled steak are unsurpassed. There are recipes in this chapter for whole steaks, steak kebabs, and also ways to handle lean and healthful venison.

Chapter 9: **Pork, Lamb, and Veal** 58
In the Southern and Gulf Coast states, pork is the most popular meat, and there are many ways to cook it, from whole slabs of ribs to the North Carolina style of barbecue. This chapter includes recipes for these popular meats, including some for skewered lamb kebabs and lean veal chops.

Chapter 10: **Burgers of All Types** 65
Today burger is no longer synonymous with beef; a burger is really any finely ground chopped food that is grilled and then served on a bun. The recipes in this chapter run the gamut from a wide variety of meat burgers to those made from poultry, fish, and legumes.

Chapter 11: **Entree Salads** 74
Entree salads are becoming increasingly popular for good reason. They are filled with healthful vegetables, and perhaps with the addition of a crust of grilled bread, they are all you need for a meal on one plate. The key to the success of these recipes is to produce salad platters or individual plates that are visually enticing, which is very easy to do with the number of colorful ingredients included.

Chapter 12: **Combination Cooking** 84
All of the recipes in this chapter—from lamb shanks to whole roasting chickens—start on the grill; they are then finished in a conventional oven. Some recipes are then roasted in a relatively cool oven to complete cooking without drying out the outer layers of meat, while others begin by being seared or smoked on the grill and are then braised to that wonderful term—fork tender. The chapter begins with charts on how to time foods cooked by these methods.

Contents

Preface

To me, grilling is more than a way of cooking; it's a way of life. The process of grilling food arouses so many sensual pleasures that the end result is more than just a meal. Perhaps that is the reason why I grill year-round; the aroma of food cooking on the grill is as welcome when bundled up against the January cold as it is when lounging in the balmy breezes of July.

Grilling is hardly an exact science; every fire, even one ignited on a gas grill, is different, just as every piece of food cooked on it is unique. The temperature of the air, the velocity and direction of the wind, and the relative humidity all have to be factored into how long it will take a grill to heat and how long it will take food to cook on it. That means that your eyes play a major role when grilling to judge what "done" means, as you poke at food to judge its texture. The sound of food searing adds aural expectation to the experience, and then there's the aroma—emerging not just from the grill but also from the food itself as the steam rises from the plate and reaches the nose.

Grilling, more than any other cooking method, provides an opportunity to share the process with those who will benefit from the results. While a few friends might keep me company in the kitchen from time to time, conventional cooking is basically a solitary endeavor. But a grill becomes the center of a social event, and hovering around it while chatting or sipping is anticipation of a meal that both the cook and the guests can enjoy. Grilling is part of Americans' way of life, especially in the Southern and Gulf Coast states highlighted in this book where the temperate climate prevails.

Most of my personal grilling has taken place in the Northeast. I currently live in Rhode Island, but I grilled on beaches and decks on Nantucket for more than a decade prior to moving here, lit many grills in tiny Georgetown courtyards while living in Washington; and spent childhood summers grilling on the sandy shores of Long Island.

However, I have traveled extensively researching American cuisine during the past twenty-five years, both its historic roots and contemporary manifestations. For many years I consulted with a television production company in New Orleans, which opened my eyes—and palate—to the exciting flavors of Creole and Cajun food.

As is the case with all of America's regional cuisines, the dishes in the Southern and Gulf Coast states developed based on the prototypes brought by immigrants when combined with available foods. While in the Northeast and Mid-Atlantic states these influences were primarily English, the South can also boast strong Spanish and French ancestry. And the factor that unites these disparate ethnic groups to create a more unified cuisine is the African influence; it was the slave cooks in the eighteenth and nineteenth centuries who cooked the dishes and integrated African ingredients and flavors into the matrix.

But this early culinary history has been tempered by the waves of immigrants who arrived from the nineteenth to twenty-first centuries, and as the size and scope of our larder is increasing exponentially with air travel and modern agricultural practices. That is why there are so many international dishes along with traditional American foods in this book; it is those foods that reflect the America of today and the various ethnic heritages that are now blended into those of the original settlers.

I hope you enjoy grilling the dishes in this book, and I hope that as you grill them you allow the pleasures of grilling to become a larger part of your life.

Ellen Brown
Providence, Rhode Island

While writing a book is a solitary endeavor, its publication is always a team effort. My thanks go to:

Eugene Brissie of The Lyons Press for envisioning such an exciting project.

Ed Claflin, my agent, for his constant support and great humor.

The talented staff at Lyons Press, especially to Ellen Urban for her knowledgeable editorial guidance, Diana Nuhn for the crash course she provided on photo selection, Sheryl Kober for her inspired design, and Jane Crosen for her eagle-eyed editing.

Constance Brown and Kenn Speiser, my dear neighbors and friends, who goodheartedly ignored the constant smoke from my grills wafting into their backyard from mine.

My many friends whose palates and culinary savvy aided me in recipe development, most especially my beloved sister, Nancy Dubler.

Tigger and Patches, my furry companions, who personally endorse all fish and seafood dishes.

Introduction

The History of Food Traditions in the Southern and Gulf Coast States

Mardi Gras parades, like this one on Canal Street in New Orleans in 1907, play an important role in the culture as well as cuisine of the Gulf Coast states.

Multiculturalism has characterized the foods of the Southern and Gulf Coast states since the arrival of the first Spanish explorers in the early 1500s. Yet these diverse culinary practices brought to the region in the seventeenth and eighteenth centuries by successive waves of English, Scots-Irish, German, French, and Italian settlers became fused into a coherent cuisine through the greatest influence of all—that of the African cooks who, as slaves, brought their foods and flavors with them to the kitchens of their masters.

Southern food ranges from seafood-based, along the large expanses of shoreline on both the warm waters of the southern Atlantic Ocean and the Gulf of Mexico, to more meat oriented in the mountainous and isolated pockets in the inland mountain regions. But regardless of location, the approach is basic; it tends to use inexpensive ingredients and simple, direct seasonings.

As is the case with every part of the country, the foundation for Southern food was what the Europeans were taught by the Native Americans who populated the land for many centuries. Yet the Native American influence is hardly monolithic, and the specific qualities of each tribe play a large role in regional diversity.

While corn was first raised in Mexico, it became a common food in what we now call the United States more than four hundred years before the arrival of the first European settler. But its prevalence as the staple crop is where unanimity ends; the agricultural practices of the Choctaw tribe in what was to become Louisiana were very different from those of the Narragansett tribe of Rhode Island or the Hopi of the Southwest.

In every American region the European settlers learned from those who had cultivated the land for centuries, but what they learned varied from region to region and tribe to tribe. It was the Native Americans from the indigenous tribes that introduced the Europeans to the practice of deep-pit barbecue, which still holds a treasured place in the region's cooking, with pork as the meat that is traditionally included.

The climate of the South was similar to that which the slaves left in West Africa, so such foods as watermelon, rice, black-eyed peas, yams, kidney beans, eggplant, okra, collard greens, and peanuts that were the mainstay of the diet on board the slave ships quickly joined the crops cultivated by Native Americans in the fields of Southern plantations.

Although the term we now use for dishes of primarily African-American parentage is "soul food," that term did not appear until the past fifty years; it was just considered "home cooking." These simple foods were nutritionally sound, such as topping rice with stewed spicy kidney beans to create a complete protein in New Orleans' famed red beans and rice, or cooking iron-rich collard greens as a way to gain that valuable nutrient when red meat was priced beyond their means.

Bourbon Street, in the heart of New Orleans's French Quarter, was the birthplace of jazz.

It was slave labor that helped to create the Southern tradition of setting a bountiful table for guests, which always included many roasts and relishes—and a large spread of desserts, especially pies with flaky pastry crusts. Pecan pie is the most universal favorite of the region, but options also included fruit pies with peaches, shortcakes, and a lemon chess pie thickened with cornmeal.

The foods cooked in the Carolinas, Georgia, northern Florida, Alabama, and Mississippi formed a large and almost homogeneous unit, with an emphasis on using all parts of a pig and many aquatic species harvested off the coast. These were all large plantation states with little industry. Some small variations did exist, however. The area from Charleston, South Carolina, to Savannah, Georgia, is known as the Low Country; it was known for rice production and for such specialties as she-crab soup, a variation on bisque. Another part of this region with some distinctive dishes is the southern part of Florida, especially the long string of tiny islands comprising the Florida Keys that end at Key West, which is only 90 miles from Cuba but more than 150 miles from Miami. Foods and crops in this part of the state are more indebted to the Caribbean islands and Cuba than to classic European cuisines.

The state of Louisiana, in which the climate is similar to that of adjoining Alabama and Mississippi, developed two distinct cuisines: that of the Cajuns in the countryside, and that of the Creoles in the city of New Orleans. Popularized by such culinary luminaries as Paul Prudhomme in the 1980s and Emeril Lagasse in the 1990s, these rich and sensual foods share a use of the "holy trinity" of chopped green bell peppers, onions, and celery as well as dishes thickened by a mixture of fat and flour called a *roux* in classic French cooking; but it is there that the similarities end.

The Cajun people of the bayous are descendants of the French-speaking inhabitants of Acadia, which is now the Canadian province of Nova Scotia, who were deported by the British and began to float down the Mississippi River to Louisiana in large numbers following the Revolutionary War. Most Cajun cooking was done in huge cauldrons, and was singularly unattractive visually although imbued with heavenly flavors.

Creole cuisine is associated with the fine restaurants of New Orleans; it combines classic European cooking methods with ingredients of the region. Creole recipes use butter and cream, which were considered luxuries by the Cajun cooks who use pork fat. Cajun cooking is spicier than Creole, and Creole chefs use far more tomatoes than their Cajun counterparts.

Southern cooking encompasses a few inland states as well as those on the coasts. Kentucky, Tennessee, West Virginia, and Arkansas share a mountainous terrain of the Ozark, Smoky, and Appalachian mountain ranges, all of which had poor soil. Except for a few fish from local streams, the mainstay of the diet was furred and feathered game that was hunted. Vegetables were simple preparations of collard greens and beans cooked for many hours with a piece of pork fat or bacon to add flavor.

But what all these states share is a love of cornbread and biscuits; they are the mainstays of Southern cooking regardless of location.

Chapter 1

Grilling Fundamentals

The unifying factor to most of the recipes in this book—excluding many desserts and side dishes—is that at some point food comes into contact with a grill. This chapter introduces you to the basic equipment and techniques used when grilling food.

Charcoal Grills

All charcoal grills have two grates; the lower grate holds the charcoal and the upper grate holds the food. Charcoal briquettes or hardwood charcoal rest on the lower grate, and once they are lit you can move them around to create the heat pattern that is best for each recipe.

Unlike conventional cooking, grills can be set up anywhere—including on secluded beaches.

The temperature of the fire is controlled by opening and closing the top and bottom vents. The more these vents are open, the hotter the fire will be, and the more they are closed, the cooler the fire.

Charcoal briquettes are the fuel used overwhelmingly by charcoal grillers, accounting for almost 90 percent of the charcoal purchased in 2007. Invented by automotive pioneer Henry Ford, briquettes are made of low-quality, powdered charcoal and binders that are compressed and molded into little black pillows.

An alternative to briquettes is hardwood charcoal, created by burning hardwood in a furnace using very little oxygen. A piece of hardwood charcoal is almost pure carbon, and has neither glue nor additives present. While almost double the cost of generic briquettes, it does burn hotter and the fire can be controlled more effectively than using briquettes.

Starting a charcoal fire is hardly difficult, and depending on how many accoutrements you want to buy, you can accomplish the job with very little effort. Here is a summary of the primary ways charcoal fires are lighted:

- **Lighter fluid.** This petroleum product is very volatile, and should be used with extreme caution. Arrange charcoal in a pyramid in the center of your grill, and spray the coals evenly with the fluid until saturated. Allow the liquid to penetrate for 1 minute, and then light the coals in locations all around the base of the pyramid with a long match or a long-handled butane lighter. *Never use additional lighter fluid once the coals have been initially lit and are smoldering.*

- **Self-starting charcoal briquettes.** These are briquettes that are pre-soaked so only lighting

One of the great twentieth-century innovations was the covered kettle grill

Tips for All Charcoal Grills

While charcoal grills range from small ones designed for picnics to ones encased in extravagant outdoor kitchens, certain rules apply. The key to success when grilling over charcoal is how well the fire is built, and then how well it is maintained if grilling for a long duration. Here are some of considerations for all charcoal fires:

- **Use enough charcoal.** This is perhaps the most common foible of charcoal grilling, regardless if the food to be grilled is a lowly hotdog or a luxurious tenderloin of beef. Make sure the fire is 4 inches larger in diameter than the food to be cooked over it. The higher the charcoal is banked, the hotter the fire will be. If you want to cook over a very hot fire, build the coals to within 3 inches of the grate on which the food will cook. Determine the amount of charcoal you need by piling it up under the cooking grate, and then push it into a pyramid for easy lighting or place it in a chimney.

Charcoal briquettes are stacked up in a chimney starter, with newspaper stuffed into the bottom chamber for fuel.

is necessary. My suggestion is to start with ten to twelve pre-soaked briquettes, and once they are flaming add conventional charcoal on top. Your food is less likely to develop the petroleum taste associated with lighter fluid.

- **Chimney charcoal lighter.** These are becoming increasingly popular because they do not involve petroleum, but they are a problem to take along for a cookout away from the house because of their bulky size. They are essentially a metal tube with a handle on one side. Inside is a grate to hold the charcoal and a chamber underneath for crumpled newspaper. Light the newspaper using a match or lighter, and set the chimney on the grill grate. The chimney effect takes the newspaper's flames up through the charcoal and lights it. When a white ash forms on the charcoal, pour the lighted coals out onto the charcoal grate.

- **Make sure the charcoal is ready.** Whether using briquettes or hardwood charcoal, the visual sign is that all pieces are lightly covered with gray ash. This means that the charcoal is fully lit and hot.

- **Clean out the ashes regularly.** The heat of a charcoal fire can be diminished if the bottom vents are clogged with ashes. Remove both grates, close the bottom vents, and scoop out the ashes. Remember to open the vents before lighting the next batch of charcoal.

- **Close down the grill after cooking.** There is no reason to waste charcoal, so close the top and bottom vents on the grill to shut it off. The half-used charcoal can be placed off to the side and used to refresh the next fire.

Gas Grills

There is no question that a gas grill is more convenient than cooking with charcoal. Lighting a gas grill is like lighting the oven broiler, and gas grills offer unparalleled convenience. Many people believe, however, that what is lost is some of the flavor and aroma transferred to food when cooking on a charcoal grill.

Gas grills use natural or LP gas for heat and flames, so the fire is efficient. Here is how to light most of them, although you should always consult the manufacturer's instructions: Open the cover, and then open the valve of the gas tank. One at a time, turn the controls to high and ignite the corresponding burner with either a long butane lighter, a long match, or the burner's own electronic ignition. Close the cover and wait 15 to 20 minutes for your grill to reach its highest heat.

Gas grills are becoming increasingly popular due to the convenience of merely turning on a burner.

Stopping a gas grill is just as easy as lighting one. Turn off each burner, and close off the gas valve. Then turn one of the burners on high for 15 seconds to bleed any gas remaining in the line, turn that burner off, and close the cover.

Tips for All Gas Grills

Gas grills are convenient, but there are also some innate safety problems because you are cooking with a highly volatile liquid. Here are some considerations for safety as well as achieving the best flavor:

- **Always keep the lid down except if expressly told to leave it open in a recipe.** Gas burns cleanly, so no residue accumulates on the interior of the lid from high-heat cooking.

- **Remove the warming rack, assuming the grill has one, before lighting the grill.** Unless you plan to actually use it, the warming rack gets in the way of turning food at the back of the grate, and can burn your hand as you try.

- **Do not skimp on the preheating time.** It is easy to know when a charcoal fire is ready for cooking, and with a gas grill your only clue is how long it has been heating. Give it a full 15 minutes, and longer in cold weather.

- **Store propane tanks—full or empty—in a well-ventilated space.** They should *never* be placed in a garage or basement.

Grilling Accessories

Gourmet shops and web sites are filled with grilling accessories, but there are only a few that are really necessary. Here is a brief list of ones I find useful:

- **A spray bottle.** For problems to be serious enough that a fire extinguisher is necessary is not common; however, minor flare-ups caused by fat dripping onto either charcoal or metal bars are a routine occurrence when grilling. A spray bottle—either purchased for the grill or a well-washed-out one from a cleaning product—is important to keep around at all times. You can target the flames without disturbing the food above them.

- **Stainless-steel tongs.** You should have a few pairs of tongs, with handles at least 12 inches long. Use tongs and not a meat fork for turning food (a meat fork causes food to lose juice and become dry).

- **Spatula.** A long-handled spatula makes flipping hamburgers and moving other foods easy.

- **Grill brush.** Use a grill brush to clean the grate on which the food sits. I clean it once at the end of grilling, and then again before adding food the next time.

- **Instant-read thermometer.** This piece of inexpensive equipment should be mandatory in every kitchen, not only for grilling but for roasting as well. All you have to do is stick it into the thickest part of food and leave it in for 20 seconds, and it registers an accurate reading on the doneness of your food.

- **Metal and bamboo skewers.** While metal skewers are indestructible, they are not as aesthetically pleasing as delicate ones made from bamboo.

Using Wood Chips for Flavor

Wood chips made from aromatic woods like hickory, mesquite, apple, and cherry add immeasurably to the flavor of grilled foods, as well as giving the skin of poultry a rich mahogany color. For charcoal grills, the secret is to soak the chips in water to cover for at least 30 minutes. Even though it is not as pronounced a flavor, you can also use wood chips on a gas grill. Place about 2 cups dry wood chips in the center of a large (12 x 18-inch) piece of heavy-duty aluminum foil. Bring up the foil on all sides and roll the ends together to seal the pouch. Poke several small holes in the top of the packet. Once the grill is hot, place the wood chip pouch under the grate across the burner shields. Smoke will eventually emerge from the holes.

Long handles are the primary requirement for cooking tools used at the grill.

Fire Configurations for Grilling

Each recipe in this book contains information about the appropriate temperature and configuration of the grill for the success of the recipe. This section guides you through what each of these mean.

- **Direct grilling.** This was how all grilling was accomplished prior to the invention of the covered kettle grill and the gas grill. The coals are lit and then evenly spread three to four layers deep on the lower grate.

- **Dual-temperature grilling.** Once the coals are ignited and have reached the desired temperature, you can customize the fire to the needs of the food. By spreading the coals so that they are three or four deep on one side of the grill and one or two layers deep on the other side, you can sear food

and then transfer it to the cooler side to complete the cooking. For a gas grill, preheat the grill on high, and then reduce half the burners to medium.

- **Indirect grilling.** When you are cooking by indirect heat on a charcoal grill, what you are actually doing is turning your covered grill into an outdoor oven. The coals are pushed to the periphery of the grill and the food is placed in the center over an aluminum drip pan rather than over direct heat. The grill is always kept covered, and the top and bottom vents are partially closed. If you have a gas grill with more than one burner, it is possible to cook over indirect heat. The grills best suited to indirect cooking are those with right and left rather than front and back burners.

Determining the Temperature of a Grill

After the coals have a light coating of ash or the gas burners have been preheated, place your hand, palm-side down, about 4–5 inches above the cooking rack, and count slowly. Here are your readings to determine the temperature of the grill.

- Hot grill: 2 seconds

- Medium-hot grill: 3–4 seconds

- Medium grill: 5–6 seconds

- Medium-low grill: 7 seconds

Grilling is a high-heat cooking method, so if you can hold your hand over the coals for more than 7 seconds, it means you should be adding more coals or preheating the gas burners longer.

Preparing the Grill Grate

Once the grill grate has heated from the fire, take a stiff wire grill brush and brush it well to remove any cooked-on food remaining.

Treating the grid with oil just prior to grilling helps ensure that food will not stick. The best way to do this is to dip a paper towel in vegetable oil, and then, holding it with tongs, rub it all over the grill grate. This is an important step to good grilling.

The Timing of Recipes and How to Use This Book

There is no universal style of cookbook and recipe writing; each author approaches the task in a somewhat personal way. In order to provide you with the maximum number of recipes, the preparation of the fire refers you back to this chapter rather than using space to restate it constantly.

Each recipe is annotated with the number of servings, which is usually given as a range. If the dish is part of a multi-course meal, it can be "stretched" to feed more people; if it is an item that is one-per-person, the number of servings is finite.

"Active time," the second annotation, is the amount of hands-on prep time needed in the kitchen before food goes to the grill. In almost all cases the amount is less than 25 minutes, or less than the amount of time needed for a charcoal grill to heat properly. This is the time measurement for all the chopping, dicing, and indoor cooking.

The third annotation is "Start to finish." While grilling is a cooking method that can be considered "fast food" because it cooks with high heat, the time needed to properly light and heat the grill must always be factored into the equation; it may take only 5 minutes to cook a pounded chicken breast, but that is *after* the grill is ready to accomplish the task.

The recipes in this book are calculated to factor in the fire preparation as part of the time necessary to complete the dish, and to be on the safe side, the assumption is 25–30 minutes.

Chapter 2

Ways to Flavor Food:
Rubs, Pastes, Marinades, and Brines

There are basically four ways to flavor food before it goes on the grill—rubs, pastes, marinades, and brines—and the amount of time required to impart flavor ranges from seconds to days. In this chapter you will find recipes and techniques for all these ways to treat food destined for the grill.

Spices, such as peppercorns and fennel seeds, should be crushed in a mortar and pestle to release their flavor.

7

Rubs

Rubs are a relatively new addition to the arsenal of ways to flavor foods, and they truly do offer flavor without fuss. Most rubs are highly concentrated mixtures of herbs and spices that should be applied to food after it has been brushed with oil. And "rub" is what you should do. Rather than just giving food a light sprinkle, the mixture should be rubbed into the food with your fingertips, at which time it is ready to grill.

---

3 tablespoons paprika

2 tablespoons garlic powder

1 tablespoon onion powder

1 tablespoon dried oregano

1 tablespoon dried thyme

2 teaspoons freshly ground black pepper

1 teaspoon cayenne

Creole Rub

Yield: ½ cup | Active time: 5 minutes | Start to finish: 5 minutes | Uses: All foods

Combine paprika, garlic powder, onion powder, oregano, thyme, pepper, and cayenne in a bowl, and mix well. Store in an airtight container in a cool, dry place for up to 1 month.

---

6 tablespoons Spanish smoked paprika

2 tablespoons ground cumin

1 tablespoon dry mustard

1 tablespoon ground turmeric

1 tablespoon dried oregano

Spanish Spice Rub

Yield: ½ cup | Active time: 5 minutes | Start to finish: 5 minutes | Uses: All foods

Combine paprika, cumin, mustard, turmeric, and oregano in a bowl, and mix well. Store in an airtight container in a cool, dry place for up to 1 month.

---

2 tablespoons chili powder

2 tablespoons paprika

1 tablespoon ground cumin

1 tablespoon ground coriander

1 tablespoon garlic powder

1 tablespoon dried oregano

1 teaspoon freshly ground black pepper

1 teaspoon crushed red pepper

South of the Border Rub

Yield: ½ cup | Active time: 5 minutes | Start to finish: 5 minutes | Uses: All foods

Combine chili powder, paprika, cumin, coriander, garlic powder, oregano, black pepper, and red pepper in a bowl, and mix well. Store in an airtight container in a cool, dry place for up to 1 month.

Steakhouse-Style Rub

Yield: ½ cup | Active time: 5 minutes | Start to finish: 5 minutes | Uses: Beef, lamb

Combine mustard, garlic powder, pepper, oregano, and basil in a bowl, and mix well. Store in an airtight container in a cool, dry place for up to 1 month.

3 tablespoons dry mustard

2 tablespoon garlic powder

2 tablespoons coarsely ground black pepper

1 tablespoon dried oregano

2 teaspoons dried basil

Aromatic Herb and Spice Rub

Yield: ½ cup | Active time: 5 minutes | Start to finish: 5 minutes | Uses: All foods

Combine coriander, thyme, cumin, pepper, oregano, and sage in a bowl, and mix well. Store in an airtight container in a cool, dry place for up to 1 month.

2 tablespoons ground coriander

2 tablespoons dried thyme

1 tablespoon ground cumin

1 tablespoon freshly ground black pepper

1 tablespoon dried oregano

1 tablespoon dried sage

Basic Herb Rub

Yield: ½ cup | Active time: 5 minutes | Start to finish: 5 minutes | Uses: All foods

Combine rosemary, thyme, sage, tarragon, and pepper in a bowl, and mix well. Store in an airtight container in a cool, dry place for up to 1 month.

3 tablespoons crumbled dried rosemary

3 tablespoons dried thyme

3 tablespoons dried sage

1 tablespoon dried tarragon

1 tablespoon freshly ground black pepper

Spices are used around the world and add vibrant color as well as flavor to foods.

Pastes

Pastes represent the middle ground between rubs and marinades, and the amount of time needed to use them is more than a rub but less than a marinade. Pastes are highly concentrated in the same way as rubs, but they also contain some perishable ingredients for accent flavors, so they are moist. Many pastes have oil added to create the proper thick texture. They should be rubbed onto meat, and allowed to sit for at least 20 minutes, or about the same amount of time it takes for a grill to heat.

---

3 tablespoons dried tarragon

2 tablespoons dried thyme

2 tablespoons grated lemon zest

4 garlic cloves, peeled and pressed through a garlic press

2 teaspoons freshly ground black pepper

3 tablespoons olive oil

Lemon-Herb Paste

Yield: ½ cup | Active time: 10 minutes | Start to finish: 10 minutes | Uses: Chicken, fish and seafood, pork, veal

Combine tarragon, thyme, lemon zest, garlic, and pepper in a bowl, and mix well. Add oil, and mix into a paste. Store in an airtight container, refrigerated, for up to 3 days.

---

3 tablespoons grated fresh ginger

5 garlic cloves, peeled and pressed through a garlic press

2 tablespoons ground cumin

2 tablespoons turmeric

1 tablespoon ground cardamom

½ teaspoon cayenne

4 tablespoons olive oil

Tandoori Paste

Yield: ½ cup | Active time: 10 minutes | Start to finish: 10 minutes | Uses: Beef, lamb, chicken, fish and seafood

Combine ginger, garlic, cumin, turmeric, cardamom, and cayenne in a bowl, and mix well. Add oil, and mix into a paste. Store in an airtight container, refrigerated, for up to 3 days.

Marinades

Marinades are a time-honored stalwart of cooking. If given enough time, food will definitely absorb the flavor, and marinades can also render less-expensive cuts of meat buttery tender. To tenderize, some sort of acid must be present. Vinegars, with the exception of rice wine and balsamic, are too strong; wines and citrus juices are far more delicate, and the food will have a complex flavor from the combination of ingredients rather than having any one dominate.

The following chart will give you some general guidelines to marinating different types of food. Keep in mind that the thinner the food, the less time is needed to achieve a meaningful flavor. Also, heartier foods require longer than delicate foods.

Marinating Foods: How Much and For How Long		
FOOD	LIQUID PER POUND	TIME
Beef	½ cup	3–24 hours
Lamb	½ cup	3–24 hours
Pork	½ cup	2–12 hours
Veal	½ cup	1–3 hours
Chicken, with skin and bones	⅓ cup	4–12 hours
Chicken breasts, boneless and skinless	⅓ cup	30 minutes–3 hours
Turkey, whole	1 cup	24 hours
Turkey breast cutlets	⅓ cup	30 minutes–3 hours
Duck, whole	½ cup	4–24 hours
Delicately flavored fish fillets (sole, halibut), and shellfish	¼ cup	30 minutes
Strongly flavored fish fillets/ steaks (tuna, bluefish)	¼–½ cup	30 minutes–1 hour
Tender vegetables (mushrooms)	¼ cup	1–2 hours
Thick-skinned vegetables (peppers, eggplant)	¼ cup	2–4 hours

Fresh herbs add their aroma and color to pastes and marinades.

¾ cup freshly squeezed orange juice

2 tablespoons freshly squeezed lime juice

2 tablespoons soy sauce

2 tablespoons chopped fresh rosemary or 2 teaspoons dried

3 garlic cloves, peeled and minced

2 tablespoons chili powder

1 tablespoon grated orange zest

Freshly ground black pepper to taste

½ cup olive oil

Spicy Citrus Marinade

Yield: 1½ cups | Active time: 10 minutes | Start to finish: 10 minutes | Uses: Beef, lamb, pork, chicken

Combine orange juice, lime juice, soy sauce, rosemary, garlic, chili powder, orange zest, and pepper in a heavy resealable plastic bag, and mix well. Add oil, and mix well again. Add food to be marinated, turning the bag to coat food evenly. Marinate food according to chart above.

Note: The marinade can be refrigerated for up to 3 days.

Jamaican Jerk Marinade

Yield: 1 cup | Active time: 15 minutes | Start to finish: 15 minutes | Uses: Pork, chicken

Combine scallions, chiles, garlic, vegetable oil, soy sauce, lime juice, allspice, sugar, thyme, cinnamon, ginger, and pepper in a food processor fitted with a steel blade or in a blender. Puree until smooth. Transfer mixture to a heavy resealable plastic bag, add food to be marinated, turning the bag to coat food evenly. Marinate food according to chart above.

Note: The marinade can be refrigerated for up to 3 days.

- 6 scallions, white parts and 3 inches of green tops, rinsed, trimmed, and sliced
- 3 jalapeño or serrano chiles, trimmed and diced
- 3 garlic cloves, peeled
- ½ cup vegetable oil
- ¼ cup soy sauce
- 2 tablespoons freshly squeezed lime juice
- 1 tablespoon ground allspice
- 2 teaspoons granulated sugar
- 1½ teaspoons dried thyme
- ½ teaspoon ground cinnamon
- ½ teaspoon ground ginger
- Freshly ground black pepper to taste

Margarita Mexican Marinade

Yield: ¾ cup | Active time: 10 minutes | Start to finish: 10 minutes | Uses: Chicken, fish and seafood

Combine lime juice, tequila, triple sec, chile, garlic, lime zest, chili powder, cumin, sugar, salt, and pepper in a heavy resealable plastic bag, and mix well. Add oil, and mix well again. Add food to be marinated, turning the bag to coat food evenly. Marinate food according to chart above.

Note: The marinade can be refrigerated for up to 3 days.

- ¼ cup freshly squeezed lime juice
- 3 tablespoons tequila
- 2 tablespoons triple sec
- 1 large jalapeño or serrano chile, seeds and ribs removed, and finely chopped
- 2 garlic cloves, peeled and minced
- 2 teaspoons grated lime zest
- 1 tablespoon chili powder
- 1 teaspoon ground cumin
- 1 teaspoon granulated sugar
- Salt and freshly ground black pepper to taste
- ¼ cup vegetable oil

¾ cup lager beer

3 tablespoons freshly squeezed lemon juice

1 tablespoon Worcestershire sauce

3 garlic cloves, peeled and minced

1 tablespoon fresh thyme or 1 teaspoon dried

Salt and hot red pepper sauce to taste

3 tablespoons olive oil

Beer Marinade

Yield: 1 cup | Active time: 5 minutes | Start to finish: 5 minutes | Uses: Chicken, fish and seafood

Combine beer, lemon juice, Worcestershire sauce, garlic, thyme, salt, and pepper sauce in a heavy resealable plastic bag, and mix well. Add oil, and mix well again. Add food to be marinated, turning the bag to coat food evenly. Marinate food according to chart above.

Note: The marinade can be refrigerated for up to 3 days.

½ cup dry red wine

2 tablespoons balsamic vinegar

2 tablespoons gin

2 tablespoons firmly packed dark brown sugar

2 tablespoons chopped fresh thyme or 2 teaspoons dried

2 tablespoons chopped fresh rosemary or 2 teaspoons dried

3 large garlic cloves, peeled and minced

2 teaspoons grated orange zest

1 teaspoon grated lemon zest

2 bay leaves, crumbled

¼ teaspoon ground cloves

Salt and freshly ground black pepper to taste

¼ cup olive oil

Hearty Red Wine Marinade

Yield: 1 cup | Active time: 10 minutes | Start to finish: 10 minutes | Uses: Beef, lamb, venison

Combine wine, vinegar, gin, brown sugar, thyme, rosemary, garlic, orange zest, lemon zest, bay leaves, cloves, salt, and pepper in a heavy resealable plastic bag, and mix well. Add oil, and mix well again. Add food to be marinated, turning the bag to coat food evenly. Marinate food according to chart above.

Note: The marinade can be refrigerated for up to 3 days.

To preserve both color and potency, spices should be kept in a cool, dry, dark place.

Lemon and Rosemary Marinade

Yield: ¾ cup | Active time: 10 minutes | Start to finish: 10 minutes | Uses: Lamb, chicken, fish and seafood

Combine lemon juice, rosemary, parsley, lemon zest, garlic, salt, and pepper in a heavy resealable plastic bag, and mix well. Add oil, and mix well again. Add food to be marinated, turning the bag to coat food evenly. Marinate food according to chart above.

Note: The marinade can be refrigerated for up to 3 days.

¼ cup freshly squeezed lemon juice

3 tablespoons chopped fresh rosemary or 1 tablespoon dried

3 tablespoons chopped fresh parsley

2 teaspoons grated lemon zest

3 garlic cloves, peeled and minced

Salt and freshly ground black pepper to taste

⅓ cup olive oil

Brines

Brining, along with smoking and salting, is the way that food was preserved prior to refrigeration and freezing. It is making a comeback today because the long soaking in flavored salty-sweet water improves the flavor and texture of foods, especially lean foods such as poultry and pork. Food, such as thin pork chops, can be brined for as little as 8 hours, while whole chickens or thick pork loins should be brined for at least 48 hours.

Apple Cider Brine

Yield: 2 quarts | Active time: 10 minutes | Start to finish: 15 minutes | Uses: Pork, chicken, turkey

1. Combine salt, sugar, apple juice concentrate, cloves, nutmeg, cinnamon, and 1 cup water in a large nonreactive saucepan, and stir well. Bring to a boil over medium-high heat, stirring occasionally. Reduce the heat to low and simmer 2 minutes.

2. Add remaining water to the pan, and allow brine to cool. Transfer brine to a large container, and add food to be brined. Cover and refrigerate.

1 cup kosher salt

½ cup granulated sugar

1 (6-ounce) can apple juice concentrate, thawed

2 tablespoons whole cloves

3 whole nutmeg, crushed

4 cinnamon sticks

7 cups cold water

1 cup kosher salt

1 cup firmly packed dark brown sugar

¼ cup fresh thyme or 2 tablespoons dried

¼ cup chopped fresh sage or 2 tablespoons dried

3 tablespoons black peppercorns

2 quarts cold water

Brown Sugar Brine

Yield: 2 quarts | Active time: 5 minutes | Start to finish: 10 minutes | Uses: Pork, chicken, turkey

1. Combine salt, brown sugar, thyme, sage, peppercorns, and 1 cup water in a large nonreactive saucepan, and stir well. Bring to a boil over medium-high heat, stirring occasionally. Reduce the heat to low and simmer 2 minutes.

2. Add remaining water to the pan, and allow brine to cool. Transfer brine to a large container, and add food to be brined. Cover and refrigerate.

Flavored vinegars add nuances to marinades and brines.

Chapter 3

Sauces for Basting and Topping

There are chapters later in this book devoted to specific dishes, many of which have sauces to top the food after it comes off the grill. The recipes in this chapter are for sauces that can be served successfully on a wide variety of foods that are grilled without one of the flavoring methods detailed in Chapter 2. The foods are simple so the sauces makes them special.

Memphis Barbecue Sauce

Yield: 2½ cups | Active time: 10 minutes | Start to finish: 25 minutes

1. Heat oil in a saucepan over medium-high heat. Add onion and garlic, and cook, stirring frequently, for 3 minutes, or until onion is translucent. Stir in paprika and cayenne, and cook for 1 minute, stirring constantly.

2. Add tomato sauce, vinegar, Worcestershire sauce, and ketchup, and bring to a boil over medium heat, whisking frequently. Reduce the heat to low and simmer sauce, uncovered, for 15 minutes. Season to taste with salt and pepper, and keep warm.

Note: The sauce can be prepared up to 3 days in advance and refrigerated, tightly covered. Reheat over low heat before using.

2 tablespoons olive oil

1 medium onion, peeled and chopped

2 garlic cloves, peeled and minced

2 tablespoons paprika

1 teaspoon cayenne or to taste

1 cup tomato sauce

1 cup cider vinegar

½ cup Worcestershire sauce

½ cup ketchup

Salt and freshly ground black pepper to taste

North Carolina Barbecue Sauce

Yield: 2 cups | Active time: 10 minutes | Start to finish: 30 minutes

1. Combine vinegar, ketchup, sugar, and red pepper flakes in a saucepan, and whisk well. Bring to a boil over medium-high heat, stirring occasionally.

2. Reduce the heat to low, and simmer sauce, uncovered, for 15 minutes, stirring occasionally. Serve hot.

Note: The sauce can be made up to 1 week in advance and refrigerated, tightly covered. Reheat over low heat before using.

1½ cups cider vinegar

⅔ cup ketchup

3 tablespoons granulated sugar

2 teaspoons crushed red pepper flakes, or to taste

1 (20-ounce) bottle ketchup

1 cup cider vinegar

½ cup firmly packed dark brown sugar

5 tablespoons Worcestershire sauce

¼ cup vegetable oil

2 tablespoons dry mustard

2 garlic cloves, peeled and minced

1 tablespoon grated fresh ginger

1 lemon, thinly sliced

½ to 1 teaspoon hot red pepper sauce, or to taste

My Favorite Barbecue Sauce

Yield: 4 cups | Active time: 10 minutes | Start to finish: 40 minutes | Uses: Meat and poultry

1. Combine ketchup, vinegar, brown sugar, Worcestershire sauce, vegetable oil, mustard, garlic, ginger, lemon, and red pepper sauce in a heavy 2-quart saucepan, and bring to a boil over medium heat, stirring occasionally.

2. Reduce the heat to low and simmer sauce, uncovered, for 30 minutes, or until thick, stirring occasionally. Strain sauce, pressing with the back of a spoon to extract as much liquid as possible. Ladle the sauce into containers and refrigerate, tightly covered.

Note: The sauce can be made up to 1 week in advance and refrigerated, tightly covered. Bring it back to room temperature before serving.

My Favorite Barbecue Sauce

Instant Asian Barbecue Sauce

Yield: 2 cups | Active time: 10 minutes | Start to finish: 10 minutes | Uses: Poultry, fish and seafood, vegetables

Combine applesauce, hoisin sauce, brown sugar, ketchup, honey, rice vinegar, soy sauce, and chile paste in a mixing bowl. Whisk until smooth. Refrigerate until ready to use.

Note: The sauce can be made up to 3 days in advance and refrigerated, tightly covered.

¾ cup unsweetened applesauce

½ cup hoisin sauce*

¼ cup firmly packed dark brown sugar

6 tablespoons ketchup

2 tablespoons honey

2 tablespoons rice vinegar

1 tablespoon soy sauce

1 tablespoon Chinese chile paste with garlic,* or to taste (or hot red pepper sauce can be substituted)

* Available in the Asian aisle of most supermarkets and in specialty markets.

Horseradish Sauce

Yield: 2 cups | Active time: 10 minutes | Start to finish: 10 minutes | Uses: Beef, lamb

Combine crème fraîche, horseradish, chives, lemon juice, and thyme in a mixing bowl. Stir well, and season to taste with salt and pepper. Refrigerate until ready to use.

Note: The sauce can be made up to 3 days in advance and refrigerated, tightly covered.

1½ cups crème fraîche

½ cup prepared white horseradish

¼ cup chopped fresh chives

2 tablespoons freshly squeezed lemon juice

1 teaspoon fresh thyme or ¼ teaspoon dried

Salt and freshly ground black pepper to taste

Blue Cheese Sauce

Yield: 1½ cups | Active time: 5 minutes | Start to finish: 5 minutes | Uses: Meats, poultry, fish and seafood, vegetables

Combine mayonnaise, sour cream, and vinegar in a mixing bowl, and whisk until smooth. Stir in the blue cheese, and season to taste with salt and pepper. Refrigerate until well chilled.

Note: The sauce can be made up to 3 days in advance and refrigerated, tightly covered.

¾ cup mayonnaise

½ cup sour cream

2 tablespoons white wine vinegar

⅓ pound blue cheese, crumbled

Salt and freshly ground black pepper to taste

19

1½ cups mayonnaise

¼ cup finely chopped cornichon, or other small sweet pickles

3 tablespoons small capers, drained, rinsed, and chopped

2 tablespoons white wine vinegar

2 tablespoons finely chopped shallot

2 tablespoons chopped fresh parsley

1 tablespoon chopped fresh tarragon or 1 teaspoon dried tarragon

Salt and freshly ground black pepper to taste

Tartar Sauce

Yield: 2 cups | Active time: 10 minutes | Start to finish: 10 minutes | Uses: Fish and seafood, vegetables

Combine mayonnaise, cornichon, capers, vinegar, shallot, parsley, and tarragon in a mixing bowl. Whisk well, and season to taste with salt and pepper. Refrigerate until ready to use.

Note: The sauce can be made up to 3 days in advance and refrigerated, tightly covered. Bring it back to room temperature before serving.

½ pound mild feta cheese, diced

½ cup sour cream

¼ cup plain whole milk yogurt, preferably Greek

¼ cup extra-virgin olive oil

2 tablespoons freshly squeezed lemon juice

2 garlic cloves, peeled

¼ cup chopped fresh dill or 2 tablespoons dried

Salt and freshly ground black pepper to taste

Greek Feta Sauce

Yield: 1½ cups | Active time: 10 minutes | Start to finish: 10 minutes | Uses: Fish, poultry, vegetables

Combine feta, sour cream, yogurt, olive oil, lemon juice, and garlic in a food processor fitted with a steel blade or in a blender. Puree until smooth. Scrape mixture into a mixing bowl, and stir in dill. Season to taste with salt and pepper, and refrigerate sauce until ready to use.

Note: The sauce can be made up to 3 days in advance and refrigerated, tightly covered.

1 cup chunky peanut butter

½ cup very hot tap water

½ cup firmly packed dark brown sugar

⅓ cup freshly squeezed lime juice

¼ cup soy sauce

2 tablespoons Asian sesame oil*

2 tablespoons Chinese chile paste with garlic*

6 garlic cloves, peeled and minced

3 scallions, white parts and 3 inches of green tops, rinsed, trimmed, and chopped

¼ cup chopped fresh cilantro

Spicy Thai Peanut Sauce

Yield: 2 cups | Active time: 10 minutes | Start to finish: 30 minutes, including 20 minutes for chilling | Uses: Meats, poultry, fish and seafood, vegetables

Combine peanut butter, water, brown sugar, lime juice, soy sauce, sesame oil, and chile paste in a mixing bowl. Whisk until well combined. Stir in garlic, scallions, and cilantro, and chill well before serving.

Note: The sauce can be made up to 3 days in advance and refrigerated, tightly covered.

* Available in the Asian aisle of most supermarkets and in specialty markets.

Herbed Tomato Sauce

Yield: 2 cups | Active time: 15 minutes | Start to finish: 1 hour | Uses: Meats, poultry, fish and seafood, vegetables

1. Heat olive oil in 2-quart saucepan over medium heat. Add onion and garlic and cook, stirring frequently, for 3 minutes, or until onion is translucent.

2. Add carrot, celery, tomatoes, parsley, oregano, thyme, and bay leaves. Bring to a boil, reduce heat to low, and simmer the sauce uncovered, stirring occasionally, for 40 minutes, or until slightly thickened. Season to taste with salt and red pepper flakes.

Note: The sauce can be made up to 3 days in advance and refrigerated, tightly covered. Bring back to a simmer before serving. It can also be frozen for up to 3 months.

¼ cup olive oil

1 medium onion, peeled and finely chopped

4 garlic cloves, peeled and minced

1 carrot, peeled and finely chopped

1 celery rib, trimmed and finely chopped

1 (28-ounce) can crushed tomatoes

2 tablespoons chopped fresh parsley

2 tablespoons chopped fresh oregano or 2 teaspoons dried

1 tablespoon fresh thyme or 1 teaspoon dried

2 bay leaves

Salt and red pepper flakes to taste

Herbed Tomato Sauce

21

½ medium cucumber, peeled, seeded, and finely chopped

2 ripe plum tomatoes, rinsed, cored, seeded, and finely chopped

2 scallions, white parts and 3 inches of green tops, rinsed, trimmed, and finely chopped

2 garlic cloves, peeled and minced

1 cup plain whole-milk yogurt

2 tablespoons chopped fresh dill or 2 teaspoons dried

2 tablespoons freshly squeezed lemon juice

Salt and freshly ground black pepper to taste

Dilled Cucumber Sauce

Yield: 2 cups | Active time: 10 minutes | Start to finish: 10 minutes | Uses: Meats, poultry, fish and seafood

Combine cucumber, tomatoes, scallions, garlic, yogurt, dill, and lemon juice in a mixing bowl. Stir well, and season to taste with salt and pepper. Refrigerate until ready to use.

Note: The sauce can be made up to 3 days in advance and refrigerated, tightly covered.

---

3 tablespoons olive oil

1 small onion, peeled and finely chopped

3 garlic cloves, peeled and minced

2 tablespoons chili powder

1 tablespoon ground cumin

¾ cup chicken stock or vegetable stock

1 (15-ounce) can tomato sauce

1 (4-ounce) can chopped mild green chiles, drained

¼ cup chopped fresh cilantro

Salt and freshly ground black pepper to taste

Mexican Tomato Sauce

Yield: 2 cups | Active time: 15 minutes | Start to finish: 35 minutes | Uses: Meats, poultry, fish and seafood, vegetables

1. Heat olive oil in a 2-quart heavy saucepan over medium-high heat. Add onion and garlic and cook, stirring frequently, for 3 minutes, or until onion is translucent. Reduce the heat to low, stir in chili powder and cumin, and cook, stirring constantly, for 1 minute.

2. Stir in stock, tomato sauce, and green chiles. Whisk well, bring to a boil, and simmer sauce, uncovered, for 15 minutes, stirring occasionally, or until the sauce is reduced by one-quarter.

3. Stir in cilantro, and season to taste with salt and pepper. Serve hot or at room temperature.

Note: The sauce can be made up to 3 days in advance and refrigerated, tightly covered. Bring it back to room temperature or to a simmer before serving.

Quick Green Chile Sauce

Yield: 2 cups | Active time: 10 minutes | Start to finish: 25 minutes | Uses: Meats, poultry, fish and seafood, vegetables

1. Heat olive oil in a 2-quart heavy saucepan over medium-high heat. Add onion and garlic and cook, stirring frequently, for 3 minutes, or until onion is translucent. Reduce the heat to low, stir in cumin, and cook, stirring constantly, for 1 minute.

2. Stir in chiles and stock. Whisk well, bring to a boil, and simmer, uncovered, for 15 minutes, stirring occasionally, or until reduced by one-quarter. Combine cold water and cornstarch in a small bowl, and stir to dissolve cornstarch. Add to sauce, and bring to a simmer, stirring constantly. Cook over low heat for 1–2 minutes, or until sauce thickens.

3. Stir in cilantro, and season to taste with salt and pepper. Serve hot or at room temperature.

Note: The sauce can be made up to 3 days in advance and refrigerated, tightly covered. Bring it back to room temperature or to a simmer before serving.

2 tablespoons olive oil

½ small red onion, peeled and finely chopped

2 garlic cloves, peeled and minced

1 tablespoon ground cumin

3 (4-ounce) cans chopped mild green chiles, drained

1 cup chicken stock or vegetable stock

1 tablespoon cold water

2 teaspoons cornstarch

3 tablespoons chopped fresh cilantro

Salt and freshly ground black pepper to taste

Chapter 4

Hors d'Oeuvres and Appetizers

When you have the grill lit for the main course of a meal, it only makes sense to utilize this versatile cooking tool for more than one dish. In this chapter you will find recipes for small nibbles to enjoy with a cocktail or glass of wine before dinner, as well as small first courses—most of them seafood—to serve at table. Many of the recipes in this chapter are excellent for buffet entertaining and cocktail parties too. In addition to the dishes in this chapter, also take a look at the soups and salads in Chapter 5 for other light options to begin a meal.

---

8 (8-inch) flour tortillas

1 cup pimiento-stuffed green olives

3 garlic cloves, peeled and minced

2 tablespoons chopped fresh parsley

1 tablespoon olive oil

1 tablespoon white wine vinegar

Vegetable oil spray

¼ pound thinly sliced mortadella

¼ pound thinly sliced baked ham

⅛ pound thinly sliced Genoa salami

¼ pound sliced provolone cheese

Muffuletta Quesadillas

Yield: 24 pieces | Active time: 15 minutes | Start to finish: 40 minutes

1. Prepare a medium-hot grill according to the instructions given in Chapter 1. Wrap tortillas in plastic wrap and microwave on high (100%) for 20 seconds, or until pliable.

2. Place olives in a food processor fitted with a steel blade. Finely chop, using on-and-off pulsing. Scrape olives into a small mixing bowl and add garlic, parsley, olive oil, and vinegar. Stir well, and set aside.

3. Spray 4 tortillas with vegetable oil spray, and place them sprayed-side down on a cookie sheet. Layer tortillas with mortadella, ham, salami, and provolone. Top with olive mixture.

4. Top with remaining 4 tortillas, and press with the palm of your hand or a spatula to close them firmly. Spray tops of quesadillas with vegetable oil spray.

5. Grill quesadillas, covered, for 2 minutes. Turn gently with a wide spatula and grill for an additional 2 minutes, or until brown and crisp. Remove quesadillas from the grill, and allow them to sit for 2 minutes. Then cut each into 6 sections and serve immediately.

Note: The quesadillas can be prepared 1 day in advance of grilling them.

Cuban Quesadillas

Yield: 24 pieces | Active time: 15 minutes | Start to finish: 40 minutes

1. Prepare a medium-hot grill according to the instructions given in Chapter 1. Wrap tortillas in plastic wrap and microwave on high (100%) for 20 seconds, or until pliable.

2. Spray 4 tortillas with vegetable oil spray, and place them sprayed-side down on a cookie sheet. Spread tortillas with half of the mustard, and then layer tortillas with ham and pork. Sprinkle pickle on top of meats, and top with Swiss cheese. Spread remaining mustard on top of cheese.

3. Top with remaining 4 tortillas, and press with the palm of your hand or a spatula to close them firmly. Spray tops of quesadillas with vegetable oil spray.

4. Grill quesadillas, covered, for 2 minutes. Turn gently with a wide spatula and grill for an additional 2 minutes, or until brown and crisp. Remove quesadillas from the grill, and allow them to sit for 2 minutes. Then cut each into 6 sections and serve immediately.

Note: The quesadillas can be prepared 1 day in advance of grilling them.

8 (8-inch) flour tortillas
Vegetable oil spray
¼ cup Dijon mustard
¼ pound thinly sliced baked ham
¼ pound thinly sliced roast pork
½ cup chopped dill pickle
¼ pound sliced Swiss cheese

Cuban Quesadillas

1 small red onion, peeled and halved lengthwise

¼ cup olive oil, divided

24 slices French or Italian bread, ½ inch thick

3 garlic cloves, peeled

5 ripe plum tomatoes, cored, seeded, and finely chopped

¼ cup crumbled feta cheese

¼ cup chopped black olives

2 tablespoons chopped mild green chiles, drained

1 teaspoon smoked Spanish paprika

½ teaspoon ground cumin

Salt and freshly ground black pepper to taste

Tomato and Olive Bruschetta

Yield: 24 pieces | Active time: 20 minutes | Start to finish: 50 minutes

1. Prepare a medium-hot grill according to the instructions given in Chapter 1.

2. Brush onion with olive oil. Grill onion, turning with tongs occasionally, for 12–15 minutes, or until onion is tender. Remove onion from the grill, and allow it to cool.

3. While onion grills, brush bread slices with oil, and grill for 2 minutes per side, or until toasted. Cut 1 garlic clove in half, and rub on 1 side of toast. Set aside.

4. Discarding root end, chop onion. Mince remaining 2 garlic cloves. Combine onion, garlic, tomatoes, feta, olives, chiles, paprika, cumin, and remaining olive oil in a mixing bowl. Season to taste with salt and pepper.

5. Mound topping on toast slices, and serve immediately.

Note: The topping and the toast slices can be prepared up to 3 hours in advance and kept at room temperature.

24 live oysters

3 tablespoons unsalted butter

3 scallions, white parts and 2 inches of green tops, rinsed, trimmed, and chopped

¼ cup finely chopped celery

4 cups firmly packed baby spinach leaves, rinsed and dried

2 tablespoons finely chopped fresh parsley

2 teaspoons Pernod or other anise-flavored liqueur

¼ cup plain breadcrumbs

Salt and cayenne to taste

Oysters Rockefeller

Yield: 4–6 servings | Active time: 20 minutes | Start to finish: 35 minutes

1. Prepare a medium-hot grill according to the instructions given in Chapter 1. Scrub oysters well under cold running water. Discard any that do not shut tightly while being scrubbed.

2. Melt butter in a large skillet over medium-high heat. Add scallions and celery and cook, stirring frequently, for 3 minutes, or until scallions are translucent. Raise the heat to high, and add spinach, stirring as it wilts. Cook for 1 minute. Stir in parsley and Pernod, and cook for 30 seconds. Stir in breadcrumbs, and season to taste with salt and cayenne. Set aside.

3. Place oysters on the grill with rounded side down. Grill, covered, 3–4 minutes. Remove oysters with tongs, and place on a hot pad. Remove and discard top shell with an oyster knife, being careful not to spill oyster liquor. Separate oysters from bottom shell, but do not remove oyster.

4. Top each oyster with 1 tablespoon of topping. Return oysters to grill, and grill, covered, for 2–3 minutes more, or until edges of oysters curl. Serve immediately.

VARIATION: *Large littleneck clams can be substituted for the oysters.*

Note: The topping mixture can be prepared up to 2 days in advance and refrigerated, tightly covered with plastic wrap. Allow it to reach room temperature before using.

Grilled Oysters

Yield: 4–6 servings | Active time: 15 minutes | Start to finish: 40 minutes

2 dozen live oysters

4 tablespoons unsalted butter, softened

2 garlic cloves, peeled and minced

3 tablespoons chopped fresh parsley

2 tablespoons chopped fresh chives

Salt and freshly ground black pepper to taste

1. Prepare a medium-hot grill according to the instructions that were given in Chapter 1. Scrub oysters well under cold running water. Discard any that do not shut tightly while being scrubbed.

2. Combine butter, garlic, parsley, chives, salt and pepper in a small bowl, and beat until smooth.

3. Place oysters on the grill with rounded side down. Grill, covered, 3–4 minutes. Remove oysters with tongs, and place on a hot pad. Remove and discard top shell with an oyster knife, being careful not to spill oyster liquor. Separate oysters from bottom shell, but do not remove oysters.

4. Top each oyster with 2 teaspoons seasoned butter. Return oysters to grill, and grill, covered, for 2–3 minutes more, or until edges of oysters curl. Serve immediately.

VARIATION: *Large littleneck clams can be substituted for the oysters.*

Note: The butter mixture can be prepared up to 3 days in advance and refrigerated, tightly covered with plastic wrap. Allow butter to reach room temperature before using.

Grilled Oysters

8–12 (8-inch) bamboo skewers

1½ pounds extra-large (16–20 per pound) raw shrimp, peeled and deveined

¾ cup olive oil, divided

6 garlic cloves, peeled and minced, divided

¼ cup chopped fresh oregano, divided

Salt and freshly ground black pepper to taste

¾ cup diced celery

¾ cup chopped pickled Italian gardiniera vegetables

12 pepperocini, stems removed, and chopped

4 whole canned pimientos or roasted and skinned red bell peppers

½ cup firmly packed fresh parsley leaves

½ cup white wine vinegar

2 tablespoons freshly squeezed lemon juice

4–6 cups salad greens or 6 large leaves Boston lettuce

Creole Marinated Shrimp

Yield: 4–6 servings | Active time: 20 minutes | Start to finish: 40 minutes

1. Soak bamboo skewers in warm water to cover, and prepare a medium-hot grill according to the instructions given in Chapter 1.

2. Place shrimp in a heavy resealable plastic bag, and add ¼ cup olive oil, 2 garlic cloves, 2 tablespoons oregano, salt, and pepper. Mix well, and marinate shrimp at room temperature for 20 minutes, turning the bag occasionally.

3. Combine celery, gardiniera vegetables, pepperocini, pimientos, remaining garlic, and parsley in a food processor fitted with a steel blade, and chop finely using on-and-off pulsing. Scrape mixture into a mixing bowl.

4. Combine vinegar, lemon juice, remaining oregano, salt, and pepper in a jar with a tight-fitting lid, and shake well. Add remaining olive oil, and well shake again. Add dressing to the bowl with vegetables, and set aside.

5. Remove shrimp from marinade, and discard marinade. Divide shrimp into 4–6 groups, and thread each group onto 2 parallel skewers. Grill shrimp, covered, for 2 minutes per side, or until pink and cooked through. Remove shrimp from skewers.

6. To serve, place 1 portion lettuce on each plate, and top with vegetables and shrimp.

Note: The vegetables and marinade can be prepared up to 1 day in advance and kept tightly covered in the refrigerator.

Marinated Sea Scallops

Yield: 6–8 servings | Active time: 30 minutes | Start to finish: 2 hours, including 45 minutes for marinating

1. Prepare a hot grill according to the instructions given in Chapter 1.

2. Toss scallops with 2 tablespoons oil, and season to taste with salt and pepper. Cut peel (including all white pith) from orange using a small serrated knife. Dice orange, and set aside.

3. Grill scallops, uncovered if using a charcoal grill, turning once, until just cooked through, about 5 minutes. Remove scallops from the grill, and allow them to cool. Cut scallops into quarters.

4. Combine scallops, orange, lime juice, cucumber, onion, chile, and remaining oil in a mixing bowl. Season to taste with salt and pepper, and refrigerate scallops, covered, for at least 45 minutes, or until cold.

5. Stir cilantro into scallop mixture. To serve, divide salad greens onto individual plates, and mound scallop mixture in the center.

VARIATION: *Large shrimp, or 1-inch cubes of any firm-fleshed white fish such as cod or halibut can be used in place of scallops.*

Note: The scallops can be cooked and the other mixture can be prepared up to 1 day in advance and refrigerated separately, tightly covered. Do not mix scallops into vegetable mixture more than 2 hours in advance.

2 pounds large sea scallops, rinsed and patted dry with paper towels

¼ cup olive oil, divided

Salt and freshly ground black pepper to taste

1 navel orange

¼ cup freshly squeezed lime juice

½ English cucumber, cut into ⅓-inch dice

¼ small red onion, peeled and chopped

1 small jalapeño or serrano chile, seeds and ribs removed, and finely chopped

¼ cup chopped fresh cilantro

3–4 cups mixed salad greens, rinsed and dried

4 boneless and skinless chicken breast halves

½ cup soy sauce

½ cup firmly packed dark brown sugar

¼ cup freshly squeezed lime juice

2 tablespoons Chinese chile paste with garlic*

4 garlic cloves, peeled and minced

1 tablespoon Asian sesame oil*

1 cup Spicy Thai Peanut Sauce (recipe on page 20)

* Available in the Asian aisle of most supermarkets and in specialty markets.

Chicken Satay

Yield: 36 pieces | Active time: 15 minutes | Start to finish: 3¼ hours, including 3 hours for marinating

1. Trim fat from chicken breasts and pull off tenderloins. Remove tendon from the center of each tenderloin by holding down tip with your finger and scraping away meat with the dull side of paring knife. Cut tenderloins in half, and cut the remaining chicken meat into 1-inch cubes.

2. Combine soy sauce, brown sugar, lime juice, chile paste, garlic, and sesame oil in a heavy resealable plastic bag, and blend well. Add chicken pieces and marinate, refrigerated, for 3 hours, turning the bag occasionally.

3. Prepare a medium-hot grill according to the instructions given in Chapter 1.

4. Remove chicken from marinade and discard marinade. Grill chicken pieces, uncovered if using a charcoal grill, turning pieces with tongs, for a total of 3–5 minutes or until brown and cooked through. Spear each piece of chicken with a toothpick or bamboo skewer and serve hot with a cup of Spicy Thai Peanut Sauce for dipping.

VARIATION: *Cubes of pork or beef, large shrimp, or strips of salmon can become satay as well as chicken.*

Note: The chicken can marinate for up to 6 hours, and it can be cooked 1 day in advance and refrigerated, tightly covered. Reheat it in a 350°F oven wrapped in aluminum foil for 5 to 10 minutes, or until hot.

Chicken Satay

Grilled Corn and Sausage Salad

Yield: 6–8 servings | Active time: 15 minutes | Start to finish: 1 hour

1. Prepare a medium-hot grill according to the instructions given in Chapter 1. If using a charcoal grill, soak mesquite chips in water for 30 minutes. If using a gas grill, create a packet for wood chips as described in Chapter 1.

2. Remove all but 1 layer of husks from corn and pull out the corn silks. Soak corn in cold water to cover for 10 minutes. Place wood chips on the grill. Grill corn, covered, for 10–15 minutes, turning with tongs occasionally.

3. When cool enough to handle, discard husks, and cut kernels off cobs using a sharp serrated knife.

4. Cook sausage in a frying pan over medium heat, breaking up lumps with a fork. Cook until brown. Combine sausage and its fat with corn, red and green bell peppers, and scallions in a mixing bowl.

5. Combine olive oil, lime juice, maple syrup, salt, and pepper in a jar with a tight-fitting lid. Shake well, and toss with the corn mixture. Toss with cilantro, and serve at room temperature on top of lettuce leaves.

Note: The salad can be made up to 2 days in advance and refrigerated, tightly covered with plastic wrap. Allow it to sit at room temperature for a few hours to take the chill off. Do not add the cilantro until just before serving.

---

1 cup mesquite chips

4 ears fresh corn, unshucked

¾ pound bulk pork sausage

½ cup finely chopped red bell pepper

½ cup finely chopped green bell pepper

3 scallions, white parts and 2 inches of green tops, rinsed, trimmed, and finely chopped

3 tablespoons olive oil

2 tablespoons freshly squeezed lime juice

2 tablespoons pure maple syrup

Salt and freshly ground black pepper to taste

3 tablespoons finely chopped cilantro

6–8 leaves romaine, rinsed and dried

Chapter 5

Soups and Small Vegetable Salads

Hot soups to warm you in winter or chilly soups to cool you in summer are always a welcome way to begin a meal, or a satisfying focus of a light supper or lunch. Most of the recipes in this chapter include components that spend some time cooking on the grill, so their aroma and flavor permeates the broth.

Small vegetable salads are another starter as versatile as they are delicious (for grilled salad entrees, see Chapter 11). All of the salad recipes in this chapter can become part of a buffet dinner.

---

1 cup hickory chips

4 large garlic cloves, unpeeled

8–10 medium ears fresh corn, unshucked

2 tablespoons unsalted butter

¼ cup yellow cornmeal

1 (4-ounce) can chopped mild green chiles, drained

2 cups chicken stock

2 cups milk

Salt and freshly ground black pepper to taste

Grilled Corn Soup

Yield: 6 to 8 servings | Active time: 20 minutes | Start to finish: 1 hour

1. Prepare a medium-hot grill according to the instructions given in Chapter 1. If using a charcoal grill, soak hickory chips in water for 30 minutes. If using a gas grill, create a packet for wood chips as described in Chapter 1.

2. Preheat the oven to 350°F. Bake garlic cloves for 15 minutes, and peel garlic when cool enough to handle. Set aside.

3. Remove all but 1 layer of husks from the corn, and pull out corn silks. Soak corn in cold water to cover for 10 minutes. Place mesquite chips on the grill. Grill corn, covered, for 10–15 minutes, turning with tongs occasionally. Remove corn from the grill, and when cool enough to handle, cut kernels from cobs using a sharp serrated knife.

4. Melt butter in a large saucepan, and cook kernels over low heat for 5 minutes, stirring occasionally. Remove 1 cup of kernels, and set aside. Puree remaining corn, roasted garlic, cornmeal, chiles, and stock in a food processor fitted with a steel blade or in a blender. This will probably have to be done in a few batches.

5. Combine puree with milk and heat to a boil over medium heat. Add reserved corn kernels, and season to taste with salt and pepper. Reduce the heat to low, and simmer for 5 minutes, stirring occasionally.

Note: The soup can be made up to 2 days in advance and refrigerated, tightly covered. Reheat soup slowly, but do not let it boil or reduce. After it has been chilled, it may have to be thinned with a little additional milk or stock.

Low Country She-Crab Soup

Yield: 6–8 servings | Active time: 15 minutes | Start to finish: 15 minutes

1. Place crabmeat on a dark-colored surface and pick it over carefully to get rid of any shell fragments. Set aside.

2. Melt butter in a saucepan over medium heat. Stir in flour and cook, stirring constantly, for 2 minutes. Stir in paprika and cayenne, and cook, stirring constantly, for 1 minute. Whisk in milk and sherry, and bring to a boil, stirring frequently. Reduce the heat to low, and simmer soup, uncovered, for 5 minutes, stirring occasionally.

3. Gently mix crabmeat into soup, and season to taste with salt and pepper. Serve immediately.

Note: The soup can be made up to 2 days in advance and refrigerated, tightly covered. Reheat over low heat.

2 cups lump crabmeat

3 tablespoons unsalted butter

3 tablespoons all-purpose flour

1 tablespoon paprika

¼ teaspoon cayenne

3 cups whole milk

¼ cup dry sherry

Salt and freshly ground black pepper to taste

Low Country She-Crab Soup

½ cup vegetable oil

¾ cup all-purpose flour

2 tablespoons unsalted butter

1 large onion, peeled and diced

1 large green bell pepper, seeds and ribs removed, and diced

2 celery ribs, rinsed, trimmed, and diced

5 garlic cloves, peeled and minced

4 cups fish stock or bottled clam juice

1 tablespoon fresh thyme or 1 teaspoon dried

2 bay leaves

1 pound okra, stems and tips trimmed, and thinly sliced

1 (14-ounce) can diced tomatoes, undrained

½–1 teaspoon hot red pepper sauce, or to taste

Salt and freshly ground black pepper to taste

1 pound large raw shrimp, peeled and deveined, rinsed

½ pound lump crabmeat, picked over to discard shell fragments

3 tablespoons chopped fresh parsley

2 cups cooked long-grain white rice, hot

Seafood Gumbo

Yield: 6–8 servings | Active time: 20 minutes | Start to finish: 1¼ hours

1. Preheat the oven to 450°F. Combine oil and flour in a Dutch oven, and place it in the oven. Bake roux for 20–30 minutes, or until walnut brown, stirring occasionally.

2. While roux bakes, heat butter in a large skillet over medium-high heat. Add onion, green pepper, celery, and garlic. Cook, stirring frequently, for 3 minutes, or until onion is translucent. Set aside.

3. Remove roux from the oven, and place it on the stove over medium heat. Add fish stock, and whisk constantly until mixture comes to a boil and thickens.

4. Add vegetable mixture, thyme, bay leaves, okra, and tomatoes to the pan. Season to taste with hot red pepper sauce, salt, and pepper. Bring to a boil, cover, and cook over low heat for 35–40 minutes, or until okra is very tender. Add shrimp, crabmeat, and parsley. Bring back to a boil, cover the pan, remove the pan from the heat, and allow gumbo to sit for 5 minutes. To serve, place rice in bottom of soup bowls and ladle gumbo on top.

Note: Steps 1–3 can be done up to 1 day in advance, and refrigerated. Continue to step 4 just prior to serving.

Farmer's Market Vegetable Soup

Yield: 4–6 servings | Active time: 20 minutes | Start to finish: 1 hour

1. Prepare a medium-hot grill according to the instructions given in Chapter 1.

2. Brush eggplant, zucchini, yellow squash, onion, and bell pepper slices with olive oil, reserving 1 tablespoon. Sprinkle vegetables with salt and pepper.

3. Grill vegetables, covered, for a total of 8 minutes, turning them once. Remove vegetables from the grill. Peel pepper, and then cut all vegetables into a ½-inch dice.

4. Heat remaining oil in a heavy 2-quart saucepan over medium-high heat. Add garlic, and cook, stirring constantly, for 1 minute. Add stock, tomatoes, parsley, oregano, and diced vegetables, and bring to a boil. Reduce the heat to low, and simmer soup, uncovered, for 15 minutes, stirring occasionally. Serve immediately.

Note: The soup can be made up to 2 days in advance and refrigerated, tightly covered. Reheat soup slowly, but do not let it boil or reduce.

1 Japanese eggplant, trimmed and cut lengthwise into ½-inch slices

1 zucchini, trimmed and cut lengthwise into ½-inch slices

1 yellow squash, trimmed and cut lengthwise into ½-inch slices

1 medium sweet onion such as Vidalia or Bermuda, peeled and cut into ½-inch slices

1 large red bell pepper, seeds and ribs removed, and cut lengthwise into quarters

¼ cup olive oil

Salt and freshly ground black pepper to taste

2 garlic cloves, peeled and minced

4 cups chicken stock

1 (14.5-ounce) can diced tomatoes, drained

¼ cup chopped fresh parsley

2 tablespoons chopped fresh oregano or 2 teaspoons dried

Farmer's Market Vegetable Soup

⅓ cup red wine vinegar

¼ cup freshly squeezed orange juice

3 garlic cloves, peeled and minced, divided

2 teaspoons grated orange zest

Salt and freshly ground black pepper to taste

⅔ cup olive oil, divided

1 pound ripe tomatoes, rinsed, cored and cut into ¾-inch dice

2 red, orange, or yellow bell peppers, seeds and ribs removed, and cut into 1-inch strips

1 pound zucchini, rinsed, trimmed, and cut on the diagonal into ⅓-inch slices

1 medium red onion, peeled and cut into ¼-inch slices

1 (12-ounce) loaf of hearty Italian bread, cut into 1-inch slices

¼ cup chopped fresh Italian parsley

1 large egg

1 (2-ounce) tube anchovy paste

4 garlic cloves, peeled and minced

¼ cup freshly squeezed lemon juice

2 tablespoons Dijon mustard

Freshly ground black pepper to taste

¾ cup extra-virgin olive oil, divided

8 slices French bread, ½ inch thick

3 romaine hearts, rinsed, and halved lengthwise

½ cup freshly grated Parmesan cheese

Panzanella Salad

Yield: 4–6 servings | Active time: 20 minutes | Start to finish: 1 hour

1. Prepare a medium-hot grill according to the instructions given in Chapter 1.

2. Combine vinegar, orange juice, 2 garlic cloves, orange zest, salt, and pepper in a jar with a tight-fitting lid, and shake well. Add ½ cup olive oil, and shake well again. Set aside.

3. Place tomatoes in a large salad bowl, and sprinkle liberally with salt and pepper.

4. Brush pepper slices, zucchini, and onion with remaining olive oil. Rub bread slices with remaining minced garlic. Grill peppers and onion, covered, for a total of 4 minutes, and bread slices and zucchini for a total of 3 minutes, turning slices frequently, or until vegetables are tender and bread is toasted. Remove food from the grill.

5. Cut bread and vegetables into 1-inch pieces, and add to bowl with tomatoes. Toss with dressing, and allow to stand for 15 minutes. Serve immediately, sprinkled with parsley.

Note: The dressing can be prepared up to a day in advance and refrigerated; return to room temperature. Bread and vegetables can be grilled up to 4 hours in advance. Do not combine salad ingredients until 15 minutes before serving.

Grilled Caesar Salad

Yield: 4 to 6 servings | Active time: 25 minutes | Start to finish: 35 minutes

1. Prepare a medium-hot grill according to the instructions given in Chapter 1.

2. Bring a small saucepan of water to a boil over high heat. Add egg and boil for 1 minute. Remove egg from water with a slotted spoon and break it into a jar with a tight-fitting lid, scraping the inside of the shell. Add anchovy paste, garlic, lemon juice, mustard, and pepper, and shake well. Add ½ cup olive oil, and shake well again. Set aside.

3. Brush bread with remaining olive oil. Grill bread, covered, for 1 minute per side, or until toasted. Remove bread from the grill, and cut into ½-inch cubes. Place croutons in a large salad bowl.

4. Grill romaine hearts, cut-side down, for 2 minutes. Cut romaine crosswise into 1-inch slices; discard cores. Add romaine to the salad bowl.

5. To serve, toss salad with as much dressing as desired. Add Parmesan, and toss again. Serve immediately.

Note: The dressing can be made up to 2 days in advance and refrigerated, tightly covered. Return to room temperature before dressing salad.

Provençal Vegetable Salad with Feta

Yield: 4–6 servings | Active time: 20 minutes | Start to finish: 1 hour

1. Combine salt and water in a large mixing bowl, and submerge eggplant slices; use a plate to press them down into the salted water. Soak eggplant for 30 minutes, then drain slices and squeeze to extract as much water as possible.

2. While eggplant soaks, prepare a medium-hot grill according to the instructions given in Chapter 1.

3. Place eggplant, zucchini, red bell pepper, onion, and mushrooms on a baking sheet, keeping vegetables segregated. Drizzle with oil and sprinkle with garlic, herbes de Provence, salt, and pepper. Turn vegetables to coat evenly.

4. Begin by placing onion and red bell pepper on the grill, and 4 minutes later add eggplant, zucchini, and mushrooms. Grill vegetables, covered, until tender and lightly brown, turning slices frequently. Vegetables should cook for a total of 10 minutes.

5. To serve, divide vegetables on individual plates or arrange on a platter. Sprinkle with vinegar, feta, olives, and basil. Serve hot or at room temperature.

Note: The vegetables can be grilled up to 4 hours in advance and kept at room temperature.

½ cup kosher salt

2 quarts cold water

2 (1-pound) eggplants, cut into ¾-inch-thick rounds

2 medium zucchini, rinsed, trimmed, and quartered lengthwise

2 red bell peppers, seeds and ribs removed, and cut into 2-inch strips

1 large sweet onion such as Vidalia or Bermuda, peeled and cut into ½-inch slices

½ pound large mushrooms, wiped clean with a damp paper towel, trimmed, and halved

⅓ cup olive oil

4 garlic cloves, peeled and minced

3 tablespoons herbes de Provence

Salt and freshly ground black pepper to taste

¼ cup balsamic vinegar

1 cup crumbled feta cheese

½ cup pitted oil-cured black olives, preferably Provençal

¼ cup firmly packed slivered fresh basil

Mixed Vegetable Salad with Oregano

Yield: 4–6 servings | Active time: 20 minutes | Start to finish: 45 minutes

1. Prepare a medium-hot grill according to the instructions given in Chapter 1.

2. Mix olive oil and garlic. Brush oil on both sides of eggplants, zucchini, yellow squash, and onion.

3. Grill vegetables, covered, for a total of 10 minutes, turning occasionally, or until crisp-tender. Remove vegetables from the grill with tongs, and, when cool enough to handle, cut vegetables into 1-inch slices.

4. To serve, divide vegetables on individual plates or arrange on a platter. Season to taste with salt and pepper, then drizzle with vinegar and sprinkle with oregano.

Note: The vegetables can be grilled up to 4 hours in advance and kept at room temperature.

⅓ cup olive oil

2 garlic cloves, peeled and minced

2 Japanese eggplants, trimmed and quartered lengthwise

1 zucchini, trimmed and quartered lengthwise

1 yellow squash, trimmed and quartered lengthwise

1 small sweet onion, such as Vidalia or Bermuda, peeled and quartered

Salt and freshly ground black pepper to taste

¼ cup balsamic vinegar

½ cup chopped fresh oregano

Chapter 6

Fish and Seafood

While shops selling only fish and seafood are disappearing from the scene, it is worth the effort to search your neighborhood for the best source you can find for fresh fish. Look for a market that offers a varied selection, that keeps its fish on foil placed on top of chipped ice, and that has a level of personal service that allows you to special-order specific varieties or cuts of fish.

Grouper with Caribbean Fruit Salsa

Southern shrimp

Southern Shrimp

Yield: 4–6 servings | Active time: 15 minutes | Start to finish: 2½ hours, including 2 hours for marinating

1. Using sharp scissors, cut along middle of the back of shrimp; leave tail and first segment intact. Devein shrimp using a sharp paring knife but do not remove shells. Rinse shrimp and pat dry with paper towels.

2. Combine shallots, garlic, lime juice, orange juice, wine, rum, soy sauce, parsley, rosemary, salt, and pepper in a heavy resealable plastic bag, and mix well. Add shrimp and marinate, refrigerated, for a minimum of 2 hours or up to 4 hours, turning the bag occasionally.

3. Prepare a medium-hot grill according to the instructions given in Chapter 1. Remove shrimp from marinade, reserving marinade. Grill shrimp, covered, for 3–4 minutes per side, or until cooked through and opaque in the center.

4. While shrimp grill, boil down marinade until it is reduced by half. Spoon a few tablespoons over each portion of shrimp. Serve immediately or at room temperature.

VARIATION: *Any firm-fleshed white fish fillet such as halibut, snapper, or cod will be just as delicious as the shrimp and will cook in the same amount of time.*

Ingredients:

- 2 pounds raw jumbo (less than 10 per pound) shrimp, unpeeled
- 2 shallots, peeled and chopped
- 2 garlic cloves, peeled and minced
- Juice of 1 lime
- ½ cup freshly squeezed orange juice
- ½ cup white wine
- 2 tablespoons dark rum
- 2 tablespoons soy sauce
- 2 tablespoons chopped fresh parsley
- 1 tablespoon chopped fresh rosemary or 1 teaspoon dried
- Salt and freshly ground black pepper to taste

8–12 (10-inch) bamboo skewers

2 pounds extra-large (16–20 per pound) raw shrimp in shells

¼ cup olive oil

3 garlic cloves, peeled and minced

Salt and freshly ground black pepper to taste

5 tablespoons unsalted butter

2 tablespoons Worcestershire sauce

2 tablespoons freshly squeezed lemon juice

3 tablespoons chopped fresh parsley

2 tablespoons paprika

1 tablespoon chili powder

1 teaspoon dried thyme

Salt to taste

1½ teaspoons freshly ground black pepper, or to taste

Barbecued Shrimp

Yield: 4–6 servings | Active time: 15 minutes | Start to finish: 40 minutes

1. Soak bamboo skewers in warm water to cover, and prepare a medium-hot grill according to the instructions given in Chapter 1.

2. Using sharp scissors, cut along middle of the back of shrimp; leave tail and first segment intact. Devein shrimp using a sharp paring knife but do not remove shells. Rinse shrimp and pat dry with paper towels. Toss shrimp with olive oil, garlic, salt, and pepper.

3. Divide shrimp into 4 groups, and thread each group onto 2 parallel skewers.

4. Melt butter in a small saucepan over medium heat. Add Worcestershire sauce, lemon juice, parsley, paprika, chili powder, thyme, salt, and pepper. Stir well, and keep warm.

5. Grill shrimp, covered, for 2–3 minutes per side, or until cooked through. Remove shrimp from skewers, and place shrimp in a mixing bowl. Pour butter sauce over shrimp, and serve immediately.

8–12 (8-inch) bamboo skewers

1½ pounds extra-large (16–20 per pound) raw shrimp, peeled and deveined

3 tablespoons olive oil

Salt and freshly ground black pepper to taste

⅓ cup mayonnaise

¼ cup grainy mustard, preferably Creole mustard

2 tablespoons freshly squeezed lemon juice

2 tablespoons chopped fresh parsley

2 tablespoons small capers, drained and rinsed

1 tablespoon prepared white horseradish

3 scallions, white parts only, rinsed, trimmed, and chopped

2 garlic cloves, peeled and minced

Shrimp Remoulade

Yield: 4–6 servings | Active time: 15 minutes | Start to finish: 35 minutes

1. Soak bamboo skewers in warm water to cover, and prepare a medium-hot grill according to the instructions given in Chapter 1.

2. Rinse shrimp and pat dry with paper towels. Rub shrimp with olive oil, and sprinkle with salt and pepper. Set aside.

3. Combine mayonnaise, mustard, lemon juice, parsley, capers, horseradish, scallions, and garlic in a mixing bowl. Whisk well, and set aside.

4. Divide shrimp into 4–6 groups, and thread each group onto 2 parallel skewers. Grill shrimp, covered, for 2 minutes per side, or until pink and cooked through. Remove shrimp from skewers. To serve, place a pool of sauce on each plate, and top it with a portion of shrimp.

VARIATION: *Any firm-fleshed white fish fillet such as halibut, snapper, or cod will be just as delicious as the shrimp and will cook in the same amount of time.*

Note: The sauce can be made up to 1 day in advance and refrigerated, tightly covered. Bring it back to room temperature before serving.

Sea Scallops with Mango Salsa and Chili Vinaigrette

Yield: 6–8 servings | Active time: 25 minutes | Start to finish: 40 minutes

1. Soak bamboo skewers in warm water to cover, and prepare a medium-hot grill according to the instructions given in Chapter 1. Rinse scallops and pat dry with paper towels.

2. Combine mango, cucumber, onion, cilantro, 1 tablespoon olive oil, and lime juice in a glass or stainless-steel mixing bowl. Stir gently, and season to taste with salt and pepper. Allow salsa to sit at room temperature for at least 15 minutes to blend flavors.

3. Combine red pepper and vinegar in a food processor fitted with a steel blade or in a blender. With the motor running, slowly add remaining olive oil and chili oil through the feed tube to emulsify dressing. Season to taste with salt and pepper, and set aside.

4. Thread scallops onto 2 parallel skewers, sprinkle with salt and pepper, and brush with vinaigrette. Grill scallops, covered, for 1½–2 minutes per side. To serve, drizzle vinaigrette over scallops and place salsa next to them on the plate.

VARIATION: *Extra-large (16 to 20 per pound) shrimp or cubes of firm-fleshed white fish like cod or swordfish can be substituted for the scallops.*

Note: Both the salsa and the dressing can be made up to 1 day in advance and refrigerated, tightly covered. Allow both to reach room temperature before serving.

Ingredients (Sea Scallops with Mango Salsa and Chili Vinaigrette):

- 12–16 (8-inch) bamboo skewers
- 2 pound sea scallops
- 1 large, ripe mango, peeled, seeded, and cut into a ¼-inch dice
- ½ small cucumber, peeled, seeded, and finely chopped
- ¼ small red onion, peeled and finely chopped
- 3 tablespoons chopped fresh cilantro
- ¾ cup olive oil, divided
- 2 tablespoons freshly squeezed lime juice
- Salt and freshly ground black pepper to taste
- 1 roasted red bell pepper, seeds and ribs removed, and finely chopped
- ⅓ cup cider vinegar
- ¼–½ teaspoon Chinese chili oil, or to taste

Sea Scallops with Garden Relish

Yield: 4–6 servings | Active time: 20 minutes | Start to finish: 40 minutes

1. Soak bamboo skewers in warm water to cover, and prepare a medium-hot grill according to the instructions given in Chapter 1.

2. Rinse scallops and pat dry with paper towels. Brush scallops with 2 tablespoons oil, and sprinkle with salt and pepper.

3. Combine tomatoes, corn, scallions, and dill in a mixing bowl. Combine vinegar, sugar, salt, and pepper in a small bowl, and stir well. Add remaining oil, and stir well again. Toss dressing with vegetables, and set aside at room temperature.

4. Thread scallops onto 2 parallel skewers. Grill scallops for 3–4 minutes per side, uncovered if using a charcoal grill. To serve, place scallops on plates, and top with relish. Serve immediately.

Note: This dish can be served either hot or cold.

Ingredients (Sea Scallops with Garden Relish):

- 8–12 (8-inch) bamboo skewers
- 24 large sea scallops
- ⅓ cup olive oil, divided
- Salt and freshly ground black pepper to taste
- 2 large ripe tomatoes, rinsed, cored, seeded, and chopped
- 1 cup fresh corn kernels, cooked
- 4 scallions, white parts and 2 inches of green tops, trimmed and thinly sliced
- 3 tablespoons chopped fresh dill
- ¼ cup white balsamic vinegar
- 2 teaspoons granulated sugar

4–6 (6–8-ounce) boneless fish steaks or fillets of your choice, at least 1 inch thick

⅔ cup commercial mayonnaise

3 tablespoons chopped fresh herbs (such as oregano, rosemary, tarragon, basil, parsley, or some combination)

2 garlic cloves, peeled and minced

Salt and freshly ground black pepper to taste

World's Easiest Fish

Yield: 4–6 servings | Active time: 15 minutes | Start to finish: 35 minutes

1. Prepare a medium-hot grill according to the instructions given in Chapter 1.

2. Rinse fish and pat dry with paper towels. Combine mayonnaise, herbs, garlic, salt, and pepper in a mixing bowl, and stir well. Coat both sides of fish steaks with mixture.

3. Grill fish, uncovered if using a charcoal grill, for 3–5 minutes per side, or until cooked through and just slightly translucent in the center. Serve immediately.

6–8 (6–8-ounce) red snapper fillets

¼ cup olive oil

Salt and freshly ground black pepper to taste

6 tablespoons (¾ stick) unsalted butter, divided

1 large onion, peeled and chopped

2 celery ribs, rinsed, trimmed, and chopped

3 garlic cloves, peeled and minced

2 cups shrimp stock or fish stock

1 (14.5-ounce) can diced tomatoes, undrained

3 tablespoons chopped fresh parsley

1 tablespoon fresh thyme or 1 teaspoon dried

2 bay leaves

1 pound crawfish tails

¼ cup all-purpose flour

Hot red pepper sauce to taste

Red Snapper with Crawfish Étouffée

Yield: 6–8 servings | Active time: 25 minutes | Start to finish: 40 minutes

1. Prepare a medium-hot grill according to the instructions given in Chapter 1.

2. Rinse fish and pat dry with paper towels. Rub fish with oil, and sprinkle with salt and pepper. Set aside.

3. Heat 3 tablespoons butter in a saucepan over medium-high heat. Add onion, celery, and garlic, and cook, stirring frequently, for 3–5 minutes, or until onion is translucent. Add shrimp stock, tomatoes, parsley, thyme, and bay leaves. Bring to a boil, reduce the heat to medium, and simmer for 10 minutes. Add crawfish, and simmer for an additional 5 minutes.

4. While sauce simmers, melt remaining 3 tablespoons butter in a small skillet over medium heat. Add flour, and cook, stirring constantly, for 2 minutes. Add flour mixture to simmering sauce after crawfish have simmered, and stir well. Cook for an additional 3 minutes, uncovered, or until thickened. Remove and discard bay leaves. Season to taste with salt, pepper, and red pepper sauce, and set aside.

5. Cook fish, uncovered if using a charcoal grill, for 4–5 minutes per side, turning gently with a wide spatula, or until fish it is opaque at the edges and slightly translucent in the center. Serve immediately, topped with sauce.

Note: If you cannot find crawfish, use tiny salad shrimp. The sauce can be prepared up to 1 day in advance and refrigerated, tightly covered. Reheat over low heat, stirring frequently.

Grouper with Caribbean Fruit Salsa

Yield: 4–6 servings | Active time: 25 minutes | Start to finish: 1½ hours, including 1 hour for salsa to blend

1. Prepare a medium-hot grill according to the instructions given in Chapter 1.

2. Rinse grouper and pat dry with paper towels. Rub fillets with 2 tablespoons olive oil, and sprinkle with salt and pepper. Combine paprika and cumin in a small bowl, and rub mixture on both sides of fillets.

3. Combine mangoes, tomato, bell pepper, cucumber, onion, chile, garlic, cilantro, lime juice, and remaining olive oil in a mixing bowl, and mix well. Season to taste with salt and pepper, and set aside at room temperature for 1 hour for the flavors to blend.

4. Grill fish, uncovered if using a charcoal grill, for 3–5 minutes per side, or until cooked through and just slightly translucent in the center. Serve immediately with each piece topped with salsa.

Note: The salsa can be prepared up to 6 hours in advance and refrigerated, tightly covered. Allow it to reach room temperature before serving.

4–6 (6–8-ounce) thick grouper fillets

⅓ cup olive oil, divided

Salt and freshly ground black pepper to taste

2 tablespoons smoked Spanish paprika

1 tablespoon ground cumin

2 ripe mangoes, peeled and finely chopped

1 medium orange tomato, rinsed, cored, seeded, and finely chopped

½ yellow bell pepper, seeds and ribs removed, and finely chopped

½ cucumber, peeled, seeded, and finely chopped

½ small red onion, peeled and finely chopped

1 small jalapeño or serrano chile, seeds and ribs removed, and finely chopped

1 garlic clove, peeled and minced

3 tablespoons chopped fresh cilantro

3 tablespoons freshly squeezed lime juice

Aegean Swordfish

Yield: 4–6 servings | Active time: 15 minutes | Start to finish: 2¼ hours, including 2 hours for marinating

1. Rinse swordfish steaks and set aside. Combine wine, lemon juice, lemon zest, garlic, shallot, parsley, oregano, thyme, salt, and pepper in a heavy resealable plastic bag, and mix well. Add olive oil, and mix well again. Add swordfish and marinate, refrigerated, for 2–3 hours, turning the bag occasionally.

2. Prepare a dual-temperature hot-and-medium grill according to the instructions given in Chapter 1.

3. Remove fish from marinade, and discard marinade. Sear fish for 2–3 minutes per side on the hot side of the grill, uncovered if using a charcoal grill, then transfer fish to the cooler side of the grill, and cook for an additional 2–3 minutes per side, or until slightly translucent in the center. Serve immediately.

VARIATION: *Other firm-fleshed fish such as sea bass, halibut, or scrod can be substituted.*

4–6 (6–8-ounce) swordfish steaks

½ cup dry white wine

¼ cup freshly squeezed lemon juice

Grated zest from 1 lemon

4 garlic cloves, peeled and minced

1 shallot, peeled and chopped

¼ cup chopped fresh parsley

2 tablespoons dried oregano

1 tablespoon fresh thyme or 1 teaspoon dried

Salt and freshly ground black pepper to taste

½ cup olive oil

4–6 (6–8-ounce) salmon fillets

2 tablespoons olive oil

Salt and freshly ground black pepper to taste

1 jalapeño or serrano chile, seeds and ribs removed

¾ cup pecans, toasted in a 350°F oven for 5 minutes

4 sprigs fresh parsley

¼ pound (1 stick) unsalted butter, softened

2 tablespoons freshly squeezed lemon juice

1⅓ cups dry white wine

4 shallots, peeled and finely chopped

⅓ cup half-and-half

Grilled Salmon with Spicy Pecan Butter

Yield: 4–6 servings | Active time: 25 minutes | Start to finish: 40 minutes

1. Prepare a medium-hot grill according to the instructions given in Chapter 1.

2. Rinse salmon, and pat dry with paper towels. Rub salmon with olive oil, sprinkle with salt and pepper, and set aside.

3. Combine jalapeño, toasted pecans, parsley, butter, and lemon juice in a food processor fitted with a steel blade, and chop finely using on-and-off pulsing. Place wine and shallots in a small saucepan and reduce by half. Add half-and-half and reduce by half again. Slowly whisk in pecan mixture, and season to taste with salt and pepper.

4. Cook fish, covered, for 4–5 minutes per side, turning gently with a wide spatula, or until fish it is opaque at the edges and slightly translucent in the center. Serve immediately, topped with butter sauce.

Note: The butter sauce can be made up to 4 hours in advance and kept hot in a warmed thermos bottle.

Chapter 7

Poultry

Famed nineteenth-century French gastronome Jean Anthelme Brillat-Savarin once wrote that "poultry is for the cook what canvas is for the painter." Its inherently mild flavor takes to myriad methods of seasoning, and it is relatively quick to cook, too.

Almost every permutation of chicken is now available in most supermarkets—from whole birds of various sizes to delicate breast tenderloins. However, there are times and reasons why knowing how to do some chicken cutting is advantageous, so here is a brief guide:

- **Pounding chicken breasts:** Some recipes will tell you to pound the breast to an even thickness so it will cook evenly and quickly. To do so, place the breast between 2 sheets of plastic wrap , and pound with the smooth side of a meat mallet or the bottom of a small, heavy skillet or saucepan.

- **Butterflying a whole chicken:** Butterflying is a process of partially boning a whole chicken so that it can be pressed down flat on the grill and will cook over direct heat, and therefore, in less time than if you kept it whole. Turn the chicken with the breast side down, and using poultry shears cut away the backbone from the tail to the head end on both sides, and discard the backbone (or save it for making stock). Open the bird by pulling the halves apart. Use a sharp paring knife to lightly score the top of the breast bone, then run your thumbs along and under the breast bone, and pull it out. Spread the bird flat. Next turn the chicken over. Cut off the wing tips, and you are ready to grill.

Tandoori Chicken Breasts

4–6 (6-ounce) boneless, skinless chicken breast halves

2 tablespoons vegetable oil

3 scallions, white parts only, rinsed, trimmed, and chopped

3 garlic cloves, peeled and minced

½ cup canned sweetened cream of coconut (not coconut milk)

½ cup freshly squeezed lime juice

2 tablespoons chopped fresh cilantro

2 tablespoons curry powder or to taste

Salt and cayenne to taste

Chicken with Curried Coconut Sauce

Yield: 4–6 servings | Active time: 20 minutes | Start to finish: 1 hour, including 30 minutes for marinating

1. Trim chicken breasts of all visible fat, and pound to an even thickness of ½ inch between 2 sheets of plastic wrap. Place chicken in a heavy resealable plastic bag, and set aside.

2. Heat oil in a small skillet over medium-high heat. Add scallions and garlic and cook, stirring frequently, for 3 minutes, or until scallions are translucent. Scrape mixture into a mixing bowl, and whisk in cream of coconut, lime juice, cilantro, curry powder, salt, and cayenne. Pour half of mixture into the bag, and mix well to coat chicken. Marinate chicken at room temperature for 30 minutes, turning the bag occasionally.

3. Prepare a hot grill according to the instructions given in Chapter 1. Remove chicken from marinade, and discard marinade.

4. Grill chicken for 2–3 minutes per side, uncovered, or until chicken is cooked through and no longer pink. Serve immediately, passing extra sauce separately.

Note: The marinade/sauce can be prepared up to 2 days in advance and refrigerated, tightly covered. Bring marinade/sauce to room temperature before serving.

4–6 (6-ounce) boneless, skinless chicken breast halves

¾ cup plain yogurt

2 tablespoons freshly squeezed lemon juice

3 garlic cloves, peeled and pressed through a garlic press

1 tablespoon grated fresh ginger

1 tablespoon ground turmeric

2 teaspoons ground coriander

1 teaspoon ground cumin

Salt and cayenne to taste

2 tablespoons vegetable oil

Tandoori Chicken Breasts

Yield: 4–6 servings | Active time: 15 minutes | Start to finish: 40 minutes, including 30 minutes for marinating

1. Prepare a hot grill according to the instructions given in Chapter 1.

2. Trim chicken breasts of all visible fat, and pound to an even thickness of ½ inch between 2 sheets of plastic wrap. Combine yogurt, lemon juice, garlic, ginger, turmeric, coriander, cumin, salt, and cayenne in a heavy resealable plastic bag. Add chicken, and marinate at room temperature for 30 minutes, turning the bag occasionally.

3. Remove chicken from marinade, and discard marinade. Pat chicken dry with paper towels, and rub with vegetable oil. Grill chicken for 2–3 minutes per side, uncovered, or until chicken is cooked through and no longer pink. Serve immediately.

Note: The marinade can be prepared up to 1 day in advance and refrigerated, tightly covered. Bring marinade to room temperature before using.

Grilled Chicken Hash

Yield: 6–8 servings | Active time: 25 minutes | Start to finish: 1 hour

1. Prepare a hot grill according to the instructions given in Chapter 1.

2. Trim chicken breasts of all visible fat, and pound to an even thickness of ½ inch between 2 sheets of plastic wrap. Place 3 tablespoons of the olive oil in a mixing bowl, and add garlic, herbes de Provence, salt, and pepper. Mix well. Add chicken breasts and stir to coat them with mixture.

3. Grill chicken for 2–3 minutes per side, uncovered, or until chicken is cooked through and no longer pink. Cut into ½-inch dice, and set aside.

4. Heat butter and remaining olive oil in a large skillet over low heat. Add onions, toss to coat with fat, and cover the pan. Cook over low heat for 10 minutes, stirring occasionally. Uncover the pan, raise the heat to medium, sprinkle with salt and stir in sugar. Cook for 20–30 minutes, stirring frequently, until onions are medium brown. If onions stick to the pan, stir to incorporate browned juices into onions.

5. While onions cook, place potatoes in a saucepan and cover with cold water. Salt water and bring potatoes to a boil over high heat. Boil for 12–15 minutes, or until very tender when tested with a knife. Drain potatoes, and mash them roughly with a potato masher. Add chicken and onions to potatoes and mix well. Season to taste with salt and pepper.

6. Preheat the oven to 450°F. Spread hash into a greased 9 x 13-inch baking pan and bake for 15 minutes, or until the top is lightly brown. Serve immediately.

Note: The hash can be prepared 2 days in advance and refrigerated, tightly covered. Reheat it, covered with aluminum foil, for 10 minutes, then remove the foil and bake for an additional 15 minutes.

4 (6-ounce) boneless, skinless chicken breast halves

⅓ cup olive oil, divided

3 garlic cloves, peeled and minced

1 tablespoon herbes de Provence

Salt and freshly ground black pepper to taste

4 tablespoons (½ stick) unsalted butter

2 large sweet onions, such as Vidalia or Bermuda, peeled and diced

1 teaspoon granulated sugar

1½ pounds small redskin potatoes, scrubbed and quartered

Chicken on the grill

4–6 (6-ounce) boneless, skinless chicken breast halves

1 cup finely chopped fresh cilantro

⅓ cup freshly squeezed lime juice

2 garlic cloves, peeled and minced

1 tablespoon ground cumin

1 tablespoon chili powder

Salt and freshly ground black pepper to taste

⅔ cup olive oil

2 bell peppers of any color, seeds and ribs removed, and quartered

2 sweet onions, such as Vidalia or Bermuda, peeled and cut into ½-inch slices

8–12 (8-inch) flour tortillas

Salsa, guacamole, sour cream (optional)

Chicken and Vegetable Fajitas

Yield: 4–6 servings | Active time: 25 minutes | Start to finish: 45 minutes, including 30 minutes for marinating

1. Prepare a hot grill according to the instructions given in Chapter 1.

2. Trim chicken breasts of all visible fat, and pound to an even thickness of ½ inch between 2 sheets of plastic wrap. Combine cilantro, lime juice, garlic, cumin, chili powder, salt, and pepper in a heavy resealable plastic bag, and mix well. Add olive oil, and mix well again. Pour off half of mixture, and set aside. Add chicken breasts to remaining marinade, and turn well to coat evenly. Marinate chicken for 30 minutes at room temperature, turning the bag occasionally.

3. While chicken marinates, grill vegetables for a total of 10–12 minutes, or until tender, turning once. Remove vegetables from the grill, and when cool enough to handle, cut into thin strips.

4. Remove chicken from marinade, and discard marinade. Grill chicken for 2–3 minutes per side, uncovered, or until chicken is cooked through and no longer pink.

5. Grill tortillas for 1 minute per side, or until grill marks show. To serve, cut chicken crosswise into thin strips, and add to vegetable mixture. Drizzle mixture with some of remaining marinade. One tortilla at a time, place a portion of mixture on the bottom edge of tortilla. Fold over one side, and roll tortilla firmly but gently to enclose filling. Serve immediately, passing salsa, guacamole, or sour cream separately, if using.

VARIATION: *For beef fajitas, substitute flank steak or skirt steak for the chicken. Marinate the beef for 2–3 hours, refrigerated. Consult a similar recipe to determine the cooking time.*

Note: Marinade can be made up to 2 days in advance and refrigerated, tightly covered.

Ham and Cheese–Stuffed Chicken

Yield: 4 servings | Active time: 15 minutes | Start to finish: 55 minutes

1. Prepare a medium-hot grill according to the instructions given in Chapter 1.

2. Rinse chicken and pat dry with paper towels. Insert a sharp paring knife into the thicker side of chicken breasts and cut a lengthwise pocket, being careful not to puncture the skin. Sprinkle chicken with salt and pepper, and set aside.

2. Combine cheese, ham, and thyme in a small bowl. Gently stuff mixture into pocket of chicken, and secure opening with a wooden toothpick or metal skewer. Combine butter, lemon juice, and Worcestershire sauce in a small bowl, and set aside.

3. Grill chicken, covered, for 10–12 minutes per side, basting it frequently with sauce. Do not baste for final 2 minutes of cooking, and discard any unused sauce. Chicken is cooked when it registers 160°F on an instant-read thermometer inserted into the thickest part. Serve immediately.

VARIATION: *Cheddar cheese and cooked sausage can be substituted for the Gruyère and ham, and either stuffing can also be used for pork chops.*

4 (10-ounce) chicken breast halves with skin and bones

Salt and freshly ground black pepper to taste

¼ pound Gruyère cheese, grated

¼ pound cooked ham, cut into ¼-inch dice

1 tablespoon fresh thyme or 1 teaspoon dried

3 tablespoons unsalted butter, melted

2 tablespoons freshly squeezed lemon juice

2 tablespoons Worcestershire sauce

Middle Eastern Chicken

Yield: 4–6 servings | Active time: 10 minutes | Start to finish: 4¾ hours, including 4 hours for marinating

1. Rinse chicken and pat dry with paper towels. Combine vinegar, onion, garlic, parsley, cumin, coriander, sugar, cinnamon, cayenne, and salt in a heavy resealable plastic bag, and mix well. Add olive oil, and mix well again. Add chicken and marinate, refrigerated, for a minimum of 4 hours, turning the bag occasionally.

2. Prepare a medium-hot grill according to the instructions given in Chapter 1.

3. Remove chicken from marinade, and discard marinade. Grill chicken, covered, for 12 minutes per side or until white meat registers 160°F and dark meat registers 180°F on an instant-read thermometer. Serve immediately.

VARIATION: *Pork chops can be substituted for the chicken pieces. Consult a similar recipe to determine the cooking time.*

4–6 chicken pieces (breasts, thighs, legs) with bones and skin

¼ cup balsamic vinegar

1 small onion, peeled and chopped

3 garlic cloves, peeled and minced

¼ cup chopped fresh parsley

3 tablespoons ground cumin

2 tablespoons ground coriander

1 tablespoon granulated sugar

1 teaspoon ground cinnamon

½ teaspoon cayenne or to taste

Salt to taste

¾ cup olive oil

2 (3-pound) whole chickens

4 bricks wrapped in heavy-duty aluminum foil

1 stick (¼ pound) unsalted butter, softened

3 tablespoons chopped fresh parsley

2 tablespoons chopped fresh rosemary or 2 teaspoons dried

1 tablespoon fresh thyme or 1 teaspoon dried

1 tablespoon grated lemon zest

Salt and freshly ground black pepper to taste

½ lemon, seeded and very thinly sliced

Butterflied Lemon-Herb Chicken

Yield: 4–6 servings | Active time: 20 minutes | Start to finish: 50 minutes

1. Rinse chickens and pat dry with paper towels. Butterfly chickens according to the instructions given above.

2. Prepare a medium-hot grill according to the instructions given in Chapter 1.

3. Combine butter, parsley, rosemary, thyme, lemon zest, salt, and pepper in a mixing bowl, and mix well. Stuff mixture under the skin of each chicken, being careful not to tear the skin. Lay lemon slices on top of herbed butter.

4. Place chickens over a medium fire skin-side down. Place 2 bricks on top of each chicken. Grill chicken, covered, for 10 minutes. Remove bricks, and turn chickens over. Replace bricks, and cook for an additional 12 minutes or until an instant-read thermometer registers 180°F when inserted into the thigh. Allow chickens to rest for 5 minutes, then cut into serving pieces, and serve immediately.

Note: Rather than using a whole chicken, you can make this dish with the individual parts of your choice. Consult a similar recipe to determine the cooking time.

6–8 turkey breast cutlets, about ½ inch thick

¼ cup olive oil, divided

2 teaspoons Italian seasoning

Salt and freshly ground black pepper to taste

¼ cup balsamic vinegar

2 garlic cloves, peeled and minced

1 tablespoon chopped fresh oregano or 1 teaspoon dried

1½ cups chopped fresh plum tomatoes

1 cup finely chopped radicchio

2 scallions, white parts only, rinsed, trimmed, and chopped

Turkey Cutlets Ensalata

Yield: 6–8 servings | Active time: 15 minutes | Start to finish: 35 minutes

1. Prepare a hot grill according to the instructions given in Chapter 1.

2. Rinse turkey and pat dry with paper towels. Rub cutlets with 1 tablespoon olive oil, and sprinkle with Italian seasoning, salt, and pepper. Set aside. Combine vinegar, garlic, oregano, salt, and pepper in a jar with a tight-fitting lid, and shake well. Add remaining olive oil, and shake well again.

3. Grill turkey for 2–3 minutes per side, uncovered, or until turkey is cooked through and no longer pink. Remove turkey from the grill, and keep warm.

4. Combine tomatoes, radicchio, and scallions in a mixing bowl. Toss with dressing. To serve, top each cutlet with a portion of salad mixture, and serve immediately.

Note: The dressing can be prepared up to 1 day in advance and refrigerated, tightly covered. Allow it to reach room temperature before using.

Asian Duck Breast

Yield: 4 servings | Active time: 20 minutes | Start to finish: 8½ hours, including 8 hours for marinating

1. Rinse duck breasts and pat dry with paper towels. Trim off all extra skin that is not covering meat, and score remaining skin with a paring knive in a small diamond pattern, being careful not to cut into the flesh beneath the skin. Combine hoisin sauce, mirin, chile paste, cilantro, scallions, garlic, ginger, salt, and pepper in a heavy resealable plastic bag, and mix well. Add duck breasts, and mix well again to coat all surfaces. Marinate duck, refrigerated, for a minimum of 8 hours or overnight, turning the bag occasionally.

2. Prepare a medium-hot grill according to the instructions given in Chapter 1.

3. Grill duck breasts skin-side down, uncovered if using a charcoal grill, for 5 minutes, or until skin is browned. Turn duck gently with tongs, and grill other side for 4–6 minutes. Remove duck from the grill, and allow it to rest for 5 minutes, lightly covered with aluminum foil. Slice each breast into ½-inch slices on the diagonal, and serve immediately.

4 (7-ounce) duck breast halves

1 cup hoisin sauce*

½ cup mirin* or sherry

1 tablespoon Chinese chile paste with garlic*

¼ cup chopped cilantro

2 scallions, white parts and 3 inches of green tops, rinsed, trimmed, and chopped

3 garlic cloves, peeled and minced

2 tablespoons grated fresh ginger

Salt and freshly ground black pepper to taste

* Available in the Asian aisle of most supermarkets and in specialty markets.

Asian Duck Breast

Chapter 8

Beef and Venison

Of course there is a chapter in this book about cooking beef—after all, steaks on the grill are part and parcel of life if you list yourself among the ranks of carnivores. Even on a gas grill, the aroma and flavor of a grilled steak is unsurpassed, even though pork is more popular in the Southern states than beef. It is only in the past few decades that farm-raised game has been available to home cooks and not just restaurant chefs. That has placed such culinary wonders as lean, healthful venison in supermarkets, and you will find some recipes for that meat in this chapter, too.

4–6 (10-ounce) New York strip or boneless rib eye steaks

2 tablespoons olive oil

5 garlic cloves, peeled and minced, divided

2 tablespoon smoked Spanish paprika

1 tablespoon dried oregano

1 teaspoon dried thyme

Salt and freshly ground black pepper to taste

2 tablespoons unsalted butter

2 cups fresh corn kernels

1 medium onion, peeled and chopped

½ red bell pepper, seeds and ribs removed, and chopped

1 cup heavy cream

Steak with Maque Choux

Yield: 4–6 servings | Active time: 25 minutes | Start to finish: 40 minutes

1. Prepare a dual-temperature hot-and-medium grill according to the instructions given in Chapter 1.

2. Rinse steaks and pat dry with paper towels. Rub steaks with olive oil. Combine 3 garlic cloves, paprika, oregano, thyme, salt, and pepper in a small bowl, and rub mixture on steaks. Set aside.

3. Heat butter in a large skillet over medium-high heat. Add corn, onion, bell pepper, and remaining garlic, and cook, stirring frequently, for 3 minutes, or until onion is translucent. Add cream, and bring to a boil. Reduce the heat to low and simmer sauce, uncovered, for 5 minutes, stirring occasionally. Keep warm.

4. Sear steaks over the hot side of the grill for 2–3 minutes per side, uncovered if using a charcoal grill. Transfer steaks to the cooler side of the grill and cook for an additional 5–7 minutes, uncovered if using a charcoal grill, or to desired doneness. Allow steaks to rest for 5 minutes. To serve place steaks on plates and top with sauce. Serve immediately.

Note: The maque choux sauce can be prepared up to 1 day in advance and refrigerated, tightly covered. Reheat it over low heat before using.

Steak with Herb Sauce

Yield: 4–6 servings | Active time: 25 minutes | Start to finish: 40 minutes

1. Prepare a dual-temperature hot-and-medium grill according to the instructions given in Chapter 1. Rinse steaks and pat dry with paper towels. Sprinkle steaks with salt and pepper.

2. Combine Worcestershire sauce, vinegar, mustard, shallots, garlic, parsley, oregano, rosemary, thyme, salt, and pepper in a jar with a tight-fitting lid, and shake well. Add olive oil, and shake well again. Set aside.

3. Sear steaks over the hot side of the grill for 2–3 minutes per side, uncovered if using a charcoal grill. Transfer steaks to the cooler side of the grill and cook for an additional 5–7 minutes, uncovered if using a charcoal grill, or to desired doneness. Allow steaks to rest for 5 minutes. To serve, slice steaks into ¾-inch slices and top with sauce. Serve immediately.

Note: The sauce can be prepared up to 1 day in advance and refrigerated, tightly covered. Allow it to reach room temperature before using.

Ingredients:

- 4–6 (10-ounce) New York strip or boneless rib eye steaks
- Salt and freshly ground black pepper to taste
- ¼ cup Worcestershire sauce
- 1 tablespoon red wine vinegar
- 1 tablespoon Dijon mustard
- 2 large shallots, peeled and minced
- 2 garlic cloves, peeled and minced
- 3 tablespoons chopped fresh parsley
- 2 tablespoons chopped fresh oregano or 2 teaspoons dried
- 1 tablespoon chopped fresh rosemary or 1 teaspoon dried
- 1 tablespoon fresh thyme or 1 teaspoon dried
- ⅓ cup extra-virgin olive oil

Steak with Marsala Mushroom Sauce

Yield: 4–6 servings | Active time: 20 minutes | Start to finish: 45 minutes

1. Prepare a dual-temperature hot-and-medium grill according to the instructions given in Chapter 1. Rinse steaks and pat dry with paper towels. Sprinkle steaks with salt and pepper.

2. Heat oil and butter in a large skillet over medium-high heat. Add shallots and garlic and cook, stirring frequently, for 3 minutes, or until shallots are translucent. Add mushrooms and cook, stirring frequently, for 5 minutes. Add marsala, stock, parsley, and thyme. Bring to a boil, and cook, stirring occasionally, until sauce is reduced by two-thirds. Season to taste with salt and pepper, and keep warm.

3. Sear steaks over the hot side of the grill for 2–3 minutes per side, uncovered if using a charcoal grill. Transfer steaks to the cooler side of the grill and cook for an additional 5–7 minutes, uncovered if using a charcoal grill, or to desired doneness. Allow steaks to rest for 5 minutes. To serve, slice steaks into ¾-inch slices and top with sauce. Serve immediately.

VARIATION: *Veal loin chops are also delicious with this sauce, as are chicken breasts.*

Note: The sauce can be prepared up to 1 day in advance and refrigerated, tightly covered. Reheat it over low heat before using.

Ingredients:

- 4–6 (10-ounce) New York strip or boneless rib eye steaks
- Salt and freshly ground black pepper to taste
- ¼ cup olive oil
- 3 tablespoons unsalted butter
- 3 shallots, peeled and minced
- 3 garlic cloves, peeled and minced
- ¾ pound mushrooms, wiped with a damp paper towel and sliced
- 1½ cups marsala wine
- ½ cup beef stock
- ¼ cup chopped fresh parsley
- 1 tablespoon fresh thyme or 1 teaspoon dried

2 (2-pound) T-bone or Porterhouse steaks, about 2 inches thick

¼ cup olive oil

5 garlic cloves, peeled and minced

2 tablespoons chopped fresh rosemary or 2 teaspoons dried

Salt and freshly ground black pepper to taste

4 tablespoons (½ stick) unsalted butter, softened

¼ cup freshly grated Parmesan cheese

1 tablespoon smoked Spanish paprika

2 teaspoons Dijon mustard

Steak with Tuscan Parmesan Butter

Yield: 4–6 servings | Active time: 20 minutes | Start to finish: 45 minutes

1. Prepare a dual-temperature hot-and-medium grill according to the instructions given in Chapter 1. Rinse steak and pat dry with paper towels.

2. Combine olive oil, garlic, rosemary, salt, and pepper in a small bowl, and mix well. Rub mixture on both sides of steaks, and set aside.

3. Combine butter, Parmesan, paprika, mustard, salt, and pepper in another small bowl, and mix well. Form mixture into a log with a sheet of plastic wrap, and chill until ready to use.

4. Sear steaks over the hot side of the grill for 2–3 minutes per side, uncovered if using a charcoal grill. Transfer steaks to the cooler side of the grill and cook for an additional 6–8 minutes, uncovered if using a charcoal grill, for rare or to desired doneness. Allow steaks to rest for 5 minutes. To serve, slice steaks into ¾-inch slices and top each serving with 1 pat of seasoned butter. Serve immediately.

Note: The butter topping can be prepared up to 1 day in advance and refrigerated, tightly covered.

Steak with Tuscan Parmesan Butter

Steak, Potato, and Mushroom Kebabs

Yield: 4–6 servings | Active time: 25 minutes | Start to finish: 3 hours, including 2 hours for marinating

1. Soak bamboo skewers in warm water to cover. Rinse beef and pat dry with paper towels. Cut beef into 1½-inch cubes. Remove and discard mushroom stems. Wipe mushrooms clean with a damp paper towel. Cut each mushroom into 8 chunks.

2. Combine wine, vinegar, garlic, rosemary, thyme, salt, and pepper in a heavy resealable plastic bag, and mix well. Add olive oil, and mix well again. Add beef and mushrooms to the bag, and marinate, refrigerated, for 2 hours or up to 4 hours, turning the bag occasionally.

3. Place potatoes in a saucepan of salted water. Bring to a boil over high heat, and boil potatoes for 10 minutes, or until barely tender. Drain potatoes, and plunge into ice water to stop the cooking action. When cool enough to handle, cut potatoes in half, or quarter them if larger than 3 inches in diameter. Set aside.

5. Prepare a dual-temperature hot-and-medium grill according to the instructions given in Chapter 1.

6. Remove meat and mushrooms from marinade, and discard marinade. Thread beef, mushroom sections, and potatoes onto 2 parallel skewers.

7. Sear kebabs on the hot side of the grill for 1½ minutes, turning them in quarter turns, uncovered if using a charcoal grill. Then transfer skewers to cooler side of the grill, and cook for a total of 6 minutes more for medium-rare or to desired doneness. Serve immediately.

VARIATION: *Cubes of boneless leg of lamb are also delicious with this recipe.*

Note: The marinade can be prepared and the potatoes can be boiled 1 day in advance and refrigerated, tightly covered.

8–12 (8-inch) bamboo skewers

2 pounds sirloin tips

2 large portobello mushrooms

¾ cup dry red wine

¼ cup balsamic vinegar

2 garlic cloves, peeled and minced

3 tablespoons chopped fresh rosemary or 1 tablespoon dried

1 tablespoon fresh thyme or 1 teaspoon dried

Salt and freshly ground black pepper to taste

⅓ cup olive oil

1 pound small new potatoes, scrubbed

1 (2-pound) flank steak

¼ cup soy sauce

¼ cup dry red wine

1 tablespoon Dijon mustard

2 tablespoons chopped fresh basil, preferably Thai basil, or 2 teaspoons dried

6 garlic cloves, peeled and minced

2 tablespoons chopped fresh cilantro

½ teaspoon crushed red pepper flakes, or to taste

Salt to taste

¼ cup olive oil

Garlicky Flank Steak

Yield: 4–6 servings | Active time: 15 minutes | Start to finish: 3½ hours, including 3 hours for marinating

1. Rinse flank steak and pat dry with paper towels. Score steak lightly on both sides with a paring knife in a diamond pattern ¼-inch deep. Combine soy sauce, wine, mustard, basil, garlic, cilantro, red pepper flakes, and salt in a heavy resealable plastic bag. Mix well, add olive oil, and mix well again. Add steak to marinade and marinate, refrigerated, for a minimum of 3 hours and up to 8 hours, turning the bag occasionally.

2. Prepare a hot grill according to the instructions given in Chapter 1.

3. Grill steak, uncovered if using a charcoal grill, for 3–4 minutes per side for medium-rare or to desired doneness. Allow steak to rest for 5 minutes, then carve into slices. Serve immediately.

Note: The marinade can be prepared up to 1 day in advance and refrigerated, tightly covered.

Garlicky Flank Steak

Venison Steaks with Red Wine Sauce

Yield: 4–6 servings | Active time: 20 minutes | Start to finish: 8½ hours, including 8 hours for marinating

1. Rinse venison and pat dry with paper towels. Place venison between 2 sheets of plastic wrap and pound to an even thickness of ⅓ inch. Combine 1½ cups wine, shallots, garlic, parsley, thyme, bay leaves, salt, and pepper in a heavy resealable plastic bag, and mix well. Add olive oil, and mix well again. Add venison, and marinate, refrigerated, for at least 8 hours or up to 24 hours, turning the bag occasionally.

2. Prepare a hot grill according to the instructions given in Chapter 1.

3. Heat 2 tablespoons butter and vegetable oil in a saucepan over medium-high heat. Add scallions and cook, stirring frequently, for 2 minutes, or until scallions are translucent. Raise the heat to high, and add remaining 1½ cups wine and brandy. Reduce over high heat, stirring occasionally, until only ⅔ cup remains. Cut remaining butter into small pieces, and whisk butter into sauce. Season to taste with salt and pepper, and set aside.

4. Remove venison from marinade and discard marinade. Sear venison for 2–3 minutes per side, uncovered if using a charcoal grill. Top steaks with sauce, and serve immediately.

Note: The sauce can be prepared up to 1 day in advance and refrigerated, tightly covered. Reheat it over low heat before using.

4–6 (6-ounce) boneless venison steaks, cut from the loin

3 cups dry red wine, divided

2 shallots, peeled and chopped

2 garlic cloves, peeled and minced

2 tablespoons chopped fresh parsley

1 tablespoon fresh thyme or 1 teaspoon dried

2 bay leaves

Salt and freshly ground black pepper to taste

½ cup olive oil

4 tablespoons (½ stick) unsalted butter, divided

2 tablespoons vegetable oil

6 scallions, white parts only, rinsed, trimmed, and chopped

2 tablespoons brandy

Chapter 9

Pork, Lamb, and Veal

When one is talking about meat in the Southern and Gulf Coast states, the animal that comes to mind is always a pig. Barbecue means pork and not beef. Ribs are pork spareribs rather than beef short ribs. And there are myriad ways that this "other white meat" is cooked as part of the Southern heritage.

Other than pork (and beef, the king of red meats), lamb is now growing in popularity in the South due to its rich flavor. Veal is still somewhat unusual to find in Southern homes—or in Southern supermarkets, for that matter.

Years ago there were butcher shops as well as butchers in every store to fulfill any special needs you might have for a cut of meat. However, that is no longer the case, so there are a few tasks formerly performed by butchers that are good to know how to do. Here are the two main ones:

- **Trimming a pork tenderloin:** Pork tenderloins usually come in packages of two, each weighing between ¾ pound and 1 pound. The first task is to use the blade of a paring knife to scrape away the fat and very thin membrane coating the entire tenderloin. After this is accomplished you will see a stripe of iridescent white running from about halfway up the tenderloin to the thick end; this is the silver skin, and it should be removed so that the tenderloin will cook without curling. It is also very tough and gristly if eaten. Hold the end of the silver skin at the thin end with one hand, and insert a paring knife under it. Scrape it away from the meat, and repeat the process until all the silver skin has been removed.

- **Butterflying a leg of lamb:** It is now rather easy to find a boneless leg of lamb, but to grill successfully it has to lie much flatter on the grill. Remove the netting encasing it, or cut the strings creating its cylindrical shape. Roll out the meat, and you will have parts of various thicknesses ranging from almost no meat to an area about 6 inches thick. Start by cutting away large areas of fat, and trim the solid fat coating, called the fell, on what would have been the top of the leg to an even thickness of ¼ inch. Holding your knife parallel to the counter, start slicing the thicker areas of the lamb, pulling them open as if you were rolling out a sheet of piecrust. When all the meat is basically flat, cover the lamb with a sheet of plastic wrap, and pound it to an even thickness of 2 inches with the bottom of a small skillet or the flat side of a meat mallet.

True North Carolina Pulled Pork Barbecue

Yield: 10–12 servings | Active time: 1 hour | Start to finish: 12 hours, including 6 hours for marinating

1. Rinse pork and pat dry with paper towels. Combine vegetable oil, garlic, onion, paprika, sugar, mustard, salt, and pepper in a small bowl. Rub paste all over pork, and refrigerate pork for a minimum of 6 hours or up to 24 hours, tightly covered with plastic wrap.

2. Prepare a fire for indirect cooking as described in Chapter 1. If using a charcoal grill, soak hickory chips in water for 30 minutes. If using a gas grill, create a packet for wood chips as described in Chapter 1.

3. Place one-third of wood chips on the grill. Place pork on the grate over a drip pan. Cover the grill and cook for 6–8 hours over low heat until it registers an internal temperature of 195°F on an instant-read thermometer, adding more charcoal hourly if using a charcoal grill and adding more wood chips hourly.

4. Remove pork from the grill, and allow it to rest for 15 minutes. Using 2 forks, shred pork into bite-sized pieces. Mix meat with North Carolina Barbecue Sauce. To serve, mound meat onto buns, and top with coleslaw. Serve immediately.

Note: The meat can be prepared up to 3 days in advance and refrigerated, tightly covered. Reheat, covered with foil, in a 350°F oven for 20–30 minutes, or until hot.

1 (6–8-pound) boneless Boston pork butt

¼ cup vegetable oil

4 garlic cloves, peeled and minced

1 small onion, peeled and chopped

2 tablespoons paprika

2 tablespoons firmly packed light brown sugar

1 tablespoon dry mustard

Salt and freshly ground black pepper to taste

2 pounds hickory chips

North Carolina Barbecue Sauce (recipe on page 17)

10–12 hamburger buns

2–3 cups coleslaw

True North Carolina Pulled Pork Barbecue

2 (¾-pound) pork
 tenderloins, trimmed
 of fat and silver skin as
 described above

⅓ cup olive oil, divided

4 garlic cloves, peeled and
 minced, divided

1 tablespoon paprika

1 tablespoon dried sage

Salt and freshly ground
 black pepper to taste

1 onion, peeled and
 chopped

½ cup orange juice

½ cup ketchup

½ cup peach preserves

¼ cup cider vinegar

1 tablespoon
 Worcestershire sauce

½ teaspoon hot red pepper
 sauce, or to taste

Peach-Glazed Pork Tenderloin

Yield: 4–6 servings | Active time: 25 minutes | Start to finish: 50 minutes

1. Place pork in a baking dish. Combine 2 tablespoons olive oil, 2 garlic cloves, paprika, sage, salt, and pepper in a small bowl, and stir well. Rub paste on pork, and allow pork to sit at room temperature while the grill heats.

2. Prepare a dual-temperature hot-and-medium grill according to the instructions given in Chapter 1.

3. Heat remaining oil in a saucepan over medium-high heat. Add onion and remaining garlic and cook, stirring frequently, for 3 minutes, or until onions are translucent. Add orange juice, ketchup, peach preserves, vinegar, and Worcestershire sauce to the pan, and whisk well. Bring to a boil, and then reduce the heat to low. Simmer sauce, uncovered, for 15 minutes, stirring occasionally. Season to taste with salt and hot red pepper sauce. Transfer one-third of sauce to a small bowl for basting pork, and keep remaining sauce warm.

4. Grill pork, uncovered if using a charcoal grill, on the hot side of the grill for 2–3 minutes per side, turning it in quarter turns, and then move pork to the cooler side of the grill. Grill for an additional 5–6 minutes per side, basting with sauce, for medium. Allow pork to rest for 5 minutes, then slice pork on the diagonal into ½-inch slices, and pass extra sauce separately.

Note: The sauce can be prepared up to 2 days in advance and refrigerated, tightly covered. Reheat it over low heat before using.

6–8 (1-inch-thick) bone-in
 pork chops

Salt and freshly ground
 black pepper to taste

5 garlic cloves, peeled and
 minced, divided

3 tablespoons ground sage

Pinch of ground allspice

2 ripe mangoes, peeled and
 coarsely chopped

⅓ cup freshly squeezed
 lime juice

1 jalapeño or serrano chile,
 seeds and ribs removed,
 and diced

1 tablespoon grated orange
 zest

2 tablespoons olive oil

3 tablespoons chopped
 fresh cilantro

Cuban Pork Chops with Mango Sauce

Yield: 6–8 servings | Active time: 15 minutes | Start to finish: 35 minutes

1. Prepare a dual-temperature hot-and-medium grill according to the instructions given in Chapter 1.

2. Rinse pork chops and pat dry with paper towels. Sprinkle pork chops with salt and pepper. Combine 2 garlic cloves, sage, and allspice in a small bowl, and rub mixture on both sides of chops.

3. Combine mangoes, lime juice, remaining garlic, chile, orange zest, and olive oil in a food processor fitted with a steel blade or in a blender. Puree until smooth. Stir in cilantro, and season to taste with salt and pepper. Set aside.

4. Grill chops, uncovered if using a charcoal grill, on the hot side of the grill for 2–3 minutes per side and then move them to the cooler side of the grill. Grill for an additional 5–6 minutes per side for medium. Allow chops to rest for 5 minutes, then serve immediately, passing sauce separately.

Note: The sauce can be made up to 2 days in advance and refrigerated, tightly covered. Bring it to room temperature before using.

Memphis-Style Ribs

Yield: 4–6 servings | Active time: 20 minutes | Start to finish: 7 hours, including 3 hours for marinating

1. Rinse ribs, and pat dry with paper towels. Cut each slab in half.

2. Combine paprika, brown sugar, granulated sugar, salt, pepper, oregano, red pepper flakes, garlic powder, mustard, and cumin in a small bowl. Rub both sides of ribs with mixture, and allow to sit at room temperature for 3 hours, or refrigerate for up to 12 hours.

3. Prepare a grill for indirect cooking as described in Chapter 1, pushing the coals to one side rather than around the periphery if using a charcoal grill, and lighting the burners on only one side if using a gas grill. If using a charcoal grill, soak hickory chips in water for 30 minutes. If using a gas grill, create a packet for wood chips as described in Chapter 1.

4. Drain wood chips, and sprinkle on coals, or place packet of wood chips under grate on burners. Place ribs on the cool side of the grill, and cook for 2 hours, covered, turning the slabs every 30 minutes to cook evenly. Add more charcoal to fire after 1 hour.

5. Move ribs to hot part of grill, and baste with barbecue sauce. Cook for 5–7 minutes per side, or until ribs are browned. Remove ribs from the grill, wrap slabs in heavy-duty aluminum foil, and allow ribs to rest for 45 minutes.

6. Reheat foil packets on the cool side of the grill, if necessary, then cut ribs into servings, and serve immediately. Pass extra sauce separately.

2 slabs pork spareribs (about 6½ pounds)

¼ cup paprika

2 tablespoons firmly packed dark brown sugar

1 tablespoon granulated sugar

1 tablespoon kosher salt

1 tablespoon freshly ground black pepper

2 teaspoons dried oregano

1½ teaspoons crushed red pepper flakes

1½ teaspoons garlic powder

1½ teaspoons dry mustard

1 teaspoon ground cumin

2 cups hickory chips

2 cups Memphis Barbecue Sauce (recipe on page 17)

2 cups hickory or mesquite chips

2 slabs pork spareribs (about 6½ pounds)

¼ cup Aromatic Herb and Spice Rub (recipe on page 9) or any spice rub of your choice

2 cups My Favorite Barbecue Sauce (recipe on page 18) or any barbecue sauce of your choice

Basic All-American Barbecued Ribs

Yield: 4–6 servings | Active time: 20 minutes | Start to finish: 4 hours

1. If using a charcoal grill, soak hickory or mesquite chips in water for 30 minutes. If using a gas grill, create a packet for wood chips as described in Chapter 1. Rinse ribs, and pat dry with paper towels. Cut each slab in half. Rub both sides of ribs with spice rub, and allow to sit at room temperature while grill heats.

2. Prepare a grill for indirect cooking as described in Chapter 1, pushing the coals to one side rather than around the periphery if using a charcoal grill, and lighting the burners on only one side if using a gas grill.

3. Drain wood chips, and sprinkle on coals, or place packet of wood chips under grate on burners. Place ribs on the cool side of the grill, and cook for 2 hours, covered, turning the slabs every 30 minutes to cook evenly. Add more charcoal to fire after 1 hour.

4. Move ribs to hot part of grill, and baste with barbecue sauce. Cook for 5–7 minutes per side, or until ribs are browned. Remove ribs from the grill, wrap slabs in heavy-duty aluminum foil, and allow ribs to rest for 45 minutes.

5. Reheat foil packets on the cool side of the grill, if necessary, then cut ribs into servings, and serve immediately. Pass extra sauce separately.

Basic All-American Barbecued Ribs

Middle Eastern Lamb Kebabs with Greek Feta Sauce

Yield: 6–8 servings | Active time: 20 minutes | Start to finish: 1½ hours, including 1 hour for marinating

1. Rinse lamb, and pat dry with paper towels. Combine wine, shallots, garlic, oregano, cinnamon, salt, and pepper in a heavy resealable plastic bag, and mix well. Add olive oil, and mix well again. Add lamb, and marinate for 1 hour at room temperature or up to 6 hours refrigerated, turning the bag occasionally.

2. Soak bamboo skewers in warm water to cover, and prepare a medium-hot grill according to the instructions given in Chapter 1.

3. Remove lamb from marinade, and discard marinade. Thread lamb onto 2 parallel skewers. Grill lamb, uncovered, for 2–3 minutes per side, turning it in quarter turns, for medium-rare. Serve immediately, passing Greek Feta Sauce separately.

3 pounds boneless leg of lamb, fat trimmed, cut into 1-inch cubes

1 cup dry red wine

2 shallots, peeled and chopped

4 garlic cloves, peeled and minced

2 tablespoons dried oregano

½ teaspoon ground cinnamon

Salt and freshly ground black pepper to taste

½ cup olive oil

12–16 (8-inch) bamboo skewers

Greek Feta Sauce (recipe on page 20)

Moroccan Lamb Chops

Yield: 4–6 servings | Active time: 15 minutes | Start to finish: 1¼ hours, including 1 hour for marinating

1. Rinse lamb and pat dry with paper towels. Combine olive oil, cilantro, garlic, paprika, coriander, cumin, salt, and pepper in a heavy resealable plastic bag, and mix well. Add chops, coating them well with mixture. Marinate chops at room temperature for 1 hour, turning the bag occasionally, or up to 6 hours refrigerated.

2. Prepare a medium-hot grill according to the instructions given in Chapter 1.

3. Remove lamb chops from marinade, and discard marinade.

4. Grill chops, covered, for 3 minutes per side for medium rare or to desired doneness. Serve immediately.

Note: The lamb chops can be grilled up to 1 day in advance and refrigerated, tightly covered. Reheat them in a single layer in a 450°F oven for 3 minutes per side, or until heated through.

2 (8-rib) racks of lamb, cut into 1-rib serving pieces

½ cup olive oil

1 cup chopped fresh cilantro

4 garlic cloves, peeled and minced

1 tablespoon paprika

1 tablespoon ground coriander

1 teaspoon ground cumin

Salt and freshly ground black pepper to taste

6 (1-inch-thick) veal chops

⅓ cup freshly squeezed lemon juice

½ cup chopped fresh parsley, divided

¼ cup chopped fresh rosemary, divided

1 tablespoon fresh thyme or 1 teaspoon dried

3 garlic cloves, peeled and minced, divided

1 shallot, peeled and chopped

Salt and freshly ground black pepper to taste

½ cup olive oil

1 tablespoon grated lemon zest

Lemon-Herb Veal Chops

Yield: 6 servings | Active time: 15 minutes | Start to finish: 4½ hours, including 4 hours for marinating

1. Rinse veal chops and pat dry with paper towels. Combine lemon juice with ¼ cup parsley, 2 tablespoons rosemary, thyme, 2 garlic cloves, shallot, salt, and pepper in a heavy resealable plastic bag, and mix well. Add olive oil, and mix well again. Add chops and marinate, refrigerated, for 4–6 hours, turning the bag occasionally.

2. While chops are marinating, combine remaining parsley, remaining rosemary, remaining garlic, and lemon zest in a small bowl. Mix well, and set aside.

3. Prepare a dual-temperature hot-and-medium grill according to the instructions given in Chapter 1.

4. Remove chops from marinade, discard marinade, and pat chops dry with paper towels. Grill chops on the hot side of the grill, uncovered if using a charcoal grill, for 3–4 minutes per side, then move them to the cooler side of the grill and cook for 4–5 minutes per side for medium or to desired doneness. Transfer chops to a platter or individual plates, and allow chops to rest for 5 minutes. Then sprinkle each with a few teaspoons of topping, and serve immediately.

VARIATION: *Thick pork chops are also delicious when soaked in this marinade.*

Lemon-Herb Veal Chops

Chapter 10

Burgers of All Types

While burger was formerly synonymous with beef, that is no longer the case. Burgers are now any food that is ground up, grilled, and placed in a bun. In this chapter you will find recipes for all types of meat, poultry, and seafood burgers, plus a vegetarian option.

Creole Shrimp Burgers

Yield: 4–6 servings | Active time: 20 minutes | Start to finish: 45 minutes

1. Prepare a dual-temperature hot-and-medium grill according to the instructions given in Chapter 1.

2. Heat oil in a large skillet over medium heat. Add onions, garlic, celery, and red bell pepper. Cook, stirring frequently, for 5 to 7 minutes, or until vegetables are soft. Scrape mixture into a mixing bowl.

3. Finely chop ½ pound shrimp, and add to the bowl. Puree remaining 1 pound shrimp in a food processor fitted with a steel blade. Add to the bowl, along with chives, parsley, hot red pepper sauce, and Cajun seasoning. Form mixture into 8–12 oval (½-inch-thick) patties.

4. Grill rolls cut-side down until toasted. Sear shrimp burgers, uncovered if using a charcoal grill, for 2 minutes per side over hot heat, and then cook for an additional 2 minutes per side over medium heat or until cooked through. Serve immediately, placing 2 patties per person on rolls with lettuce, tomato, and Tartar Sauce.

VARIATION: *Scallops or a firm-fleshed white fish such as cod or tilapia can be substituted for the shrimp. Serve immediately on rolls with lettuce, tomato, and Tartar Sauce.*

Note: The shrimp mixture can be prepared up to 1 day in advance and refrigerated, tightly covered.

2 tablespoons vegetable oil

1 small onion, peeled and chopped

2 garlic cloves, peeled and minced

1 celery rib, rinsed, trimmed, and chopped

1 red bell pepper, seeds and ribs removed, and finely chopped

1½ pounds large (21–30 per pound) raw shrimp, peeled and deveined

3 tablespoons chopped fresh chives

3 tablespoons chopped fresh parsley

½ teaspoon hot red pepper sauce or to taste

Cajun seasoning to taste

4–6 long submarine rolls, split in half

Lettuce, tomato, and Tartar Sauce (recipe on page 20)

1 pound lump crabmeat

3 tablespoons unsalted butter

8 scallions, white parts and 3 inches of green tops, rinsed, trimmed, and chopped

½ red bell pepper, seeds and ribs removed, and chopped

2 garlic cloves, peeled and minced

1 cup mayonnaise, divided

1 large egg, lightly beaten

1 tablespoon paprika

2 teaspoons Worcestershire sauce

½ teaspoon dried thyme

Salt and cayenne to taste

½ cup plain breadcrumbs

¼ cup finely chopped sweet pickle

3 tablespoons Creole mustard

4–6 rolls of your choice, sliced in half

3 tablespoons vegetable oil

Lettuce and tomato

Crabcake Burgers with Creole Mustard Sauce

Yield: 4–6 servings | Active time: 20 minutes | Start to finish: 1½ hours, including 45 minutes for chilling

1. Place crabmeat on a dark surface and pick it over carefully to discard all shell fragments. Set aside.

2. Heat butter in a small skillet over medium-high heat. Add scallions, bell pepper, and garlic, and cook, stirring frequently, for 3–5 minutes or until vegetables are soft. Set aside.

3. Combine ⅓ cup mayonnaise, egg, paprika, Worcestershire sauce, thyme, salt, and cayenne in a mixing bowl, and whisk well. Stir in breadcrumbs, and then gently fold in crab. Form crab mixture into 4–6 (¾-inch-thick) burgers. Cover burgers with plastic wrap, and refrigerate for at least 45 minutes.

4. Prepare a dual-temperature hot-and-medium grill according to the instructions given in Chapter 1. While burgers chill, combine remaining ⅔ cup mayonnaise, pickle, and mustard in a mixing bowl, and whisk well. Refrigerate until ready to use.

5. Grill rolls on the hot side of the grill cut-side down until toasted. Brush burgers with oil. Sear burgers over high heat for 2 minutes per side, uncovered if using a charcoal grill, and then transfer burgers to the cooler side of the grill. Continue to cook, covered, for 3–5 minutes per side or until burgers are cooked through. Serve immediately on rolls with sauce, lettuce, and tomato.

Note: The burgers can be formed up to 6 hours in advance and refrigerated, tightly covered.

Dilled Salmon Burgers

Yield: 4–6 servings | Active time: 20 minutes | Start to finish: 2 hours

1 (1½-pound) salmon fillet, skinned

¼ cup Dijon mustard, divided

¼ cup chopped fresh dill, divided

Salt and freshly ground black pepper to taste

¼ cup mayonnaise

¼ cup sour cream

2 tablespoons vegetable oil

4 rolls of your choice, sliced in half

Lettuce, tomato, and thinly sliced red onion

1. Rinse salmon, pat dry with paper towels, and cut into 1-inch pieces. Place salmon cubes on a sheet of plastic wrap, and freeze for 20–30 minutes, or until firm but not solid. Chop salmon in a food processor fitted with a steel blade using on-and-off pulsing. Place salmon in a mixing bowl and add 2 tablespoons mustard and 2 tablespoons dill. Season to taste with salt and pepper.

2. Form salmon mixture into 4–6 (¾-inch-thick) burgers. Cover burgers with plastic wrap, and refrigerate for at least 45 minutes.

3. Prepare a medium-hot grill according to the instructions given in Chapter 1. While burgers chill, combine mayonnaise and sour cream with remaining mustard and remaining dill. Stir well, and refrigerate until ready to use.

4. Grill rolls cut-side down until toasted. Rub burgers with oil, and grill for 3 minutes per side, covered, for a medium-rare burger or to desired doneness. Serve immediately on rolls with sauce, lettuce, tomato, and onion slices.

VARIATION: *Tuna or a firm-fleshed white fish like cod or halibut can be substituted for the salmon.*

Note: The burgers can be formed up to 6 hours in advance and refrigerated, tightly covered.

Dilled Salmon Burgers

2 tablespoons olive oil

½ small red onion, peeled and chopped

3 garlic cloves, peeled and minced

1¾ pounds ground turkey

¼ cup freshly grated Parmesan cheese

3 tablespoons chopped fresh parsley

2 tablespoons chopped fresh basil or 2 teaspoons dried

1 tablespoon chopped fresh oregano or 1 teaspoon dried

Salt and freshly ground black pepper to taste

4–6 Italian rolls, sliced in half

¼ pound whole-milk mozzarella cheese, sliced

½ cup marinara sauce

Lettuce and thinly sliced red onion

Italian Turkey Burgers

Yield: 4–6 servings | Active time: 15 minutes | Start to finish: 45 minutes

1. Prepare a dual-temperature hot-and-medium grill according to the instructions given in Chapter 1.

2. Heat olive oil in a small skillet over medium-high heat. Add onion and garlic and cook, stirring frequently, for 5 minutes, or until onion is soft. Scrape mixture into a mixing bowl. Add turkey, Parmesan cheese, parsley, basil, and oregano. Season to taste with salt and pepper. Mix thoroughly, and form mixture into 4–6 (¾-inch-thick) burgers.

3. Grill rolls on the hot side of the grill cut-side down until toasted. Sear burgers over high heat for 2 minutes per side, uncovered if using a charcoal grill, then transfer burgers to the cooler side of the grill. Continue to cook, covered, for 3–5 minutes per side or until burgers register 160°F on an instant-read thermometer and are cooked through and no longer pink.

4. Place cheese on burgers and cover grill. Cook for 2 minutes, covered, or until cheese melts. Place burgers on rolls and top with marinara sauce. Serve immediately with lettuce and red onion.

VARIATION: *Ground pork or ground veal can be substituted for the turkey. Cook these meats to desired doneness.*

Note: The turkey mixture can be prepared up to 1 day in advance and refrigerated, tightly covered.

Mexican Beef and Chorizo Burgers

Yield: 4–6 servings | Active time: 15 minutes | Start to finish: 40 minutes

1. Prepare a medium-hot grill according to the instructions given in Chapter 1.

2. Remove casings from chorizo, if necessary, and chop chorizo finely in a food processor fitted with a steel blade using on-and-off pulsing. Combine chorizo, ground chuck, shallots, 3 garlic cloves, cilantro, chili powder, cumin, and oregano in a mixing bowl. Season to taste with salt and cayenne. Mix well, and form mixture into 8–12 (⅓-inch-thick) patties. Place cheese on half of patties, and top with remaining patties. Press together gently to enclose cheese. Press with your thumb in the center of each burger to form an indentation; this keeps the burgers from creating a dome in the center.

3. Combine mayonnaise, remaining garlic, green chiles, and lime juice in a small bowl. Season with salt and cayenne to taste, and stir well. Set aside.

4. Grill rolls cut-side down until toasted. Grill burgers beginning with the side with the indentation up, uncovered if using a charcoal grill, for a total time of 4–6 minutes per side or to an internal temperature of 125˚F for medium-rare or to desired doneness. To serve, place burgers on bottom half of rolls and top each with mayonnaise. Serve immediately with lettuce, tomato, and red onion.

VARIATION: *Ground turkey can be substituted for the beef. Cook burgers to an internal temperature of 160˚F on an instant-read thermometer or until cooked through and no longer pink.*

Note: The beef mixture can be prepared up to 1 day in advance and refrigerated, tightly covered.

½ pound chorizo

1 pound ground chuck

2 shallots, peeled and finely chopped

4 garlic cloves, peeled, minced, and divided

3 tablespoons chopped fresh cilantro

2 tablespoons chili powder

2 teaspoons ground cumin

1 teaspoon dried oregano

Salt and cayenne to taste

1 cup grated jalapeño Jack cheese

¾ cup mayonnaise

2 tablespoons diced, canned, mild green chiles, drained

1 tablespoon freshly squeezed lime juice

4 rolls of your choice, sliced in half

Lettuce, tomato slices, and thinly sliced red onion

1¾ pounds ground chuck

¾ cup grated cheddar cheese

2 garlic cloves, peeled and minced

1 tablespoon fresh thyme or 1 teaspoon dried

Salt and freshly ground black pepper to taste

2 tablespoons unsalted butter

1 tablespoon olive oil

¼ pound mushrooms, wiped with a damp paper towel, trimmed, and sliced

4–6 rolls of your choice, sliced in half

4–6 slices cheddar cheese

Lettuce, tomatoes, and thinly sliced red onion

Fancy Cheese Burgers

Yield: 4–6 servings | Active time: 15 minutes | Start to finish: 40 minutes

1. Prepare a medium-hot grill according to the instructions given in Chapter 1.

2. Combine ground beef, grated cheddar cheese, garlic, thyme, salt, and pepper in a mixing bowl, and mix gently. Form mixture into 4–6 (1-inch-thick) burgers. Press with your thumb in the center of each burger to form an indentation; this keeps the burgers from creating a dome in the center.

3. Heat butter and oil in a large skillet over medium-high heat. Add mushrooms and cook, stirring frequently, for 4–5 minutes, or until mushrooms are browned. Season to taste with salt and pepper, and set aside.

4. Grill rolls cut-side down until toasted. Grill burgers beginning with the side with the indentation up, uncovered if using a charcoal grill, for a total time of 4–6 minutes per side or to an internal temperature of 125°F for medium rare or to desired doneness. Top burgers with sliced cheddar for last 2 minutes of grilling. Serve immediately, topped with mushrooms, lettuce, tomato, and onion.

VARIATION: *Ground turkey can be substituted for the beef. Cook turkey to an internal temperature of 160°F on an instant-read thermometer or until cooked through and no longer pink.*

Note: The beef mixture can be prepared up to 1 day in advance and refrigerated, tightly covered.

Fancy Cheese Burgers

Greek Lamb Burgers

Yield: 4–6 servings | Active time: 20 minutes | Start to finish: 40 minutes

1. Prepare a medium-hot grill according to the instructions given in Chapter 1.

2. Place yogurt in a strainer set over a mixing bowl. Shake strainer gently a few times, and allow yogurt to drain for at least 30 minutes at room temperature or up to 6 hours refrigerated. Discard whey from mixing bowl, and place yogurt in the bowl. Set aside.

3. Combine lamb, shallots, garlic, parsley, oregano, thyme, and cumin in a mixing bowl. Season to taste with salt and pepper. Mix well, and form mixture into 4–6 (1-inch-thick) burgers. Press with your thumb in the center of each burger to form an indentation; this keeps the burgers from creating a dome in the center.

4. Grill burgers beginning with the side with the indentation up, uncovered if using a charcoal grill, for a total time of 4–6 minutes per side or to an internal temperature of 125°F for medium-rare or to desired doneness. While burgers are grilling combine drained yogurt, cucumber, and tomatoes in a small bowl. Season to taste with salt and pepper.

5. To serve, cut top 1 inch off pita breads and place burgers inside. Spoon yogurt mixture on top of each burger in pita bread, and serve immediately.

VARIATION: *Ground beef can be substituted for the ground lamb.*

Note: The lamb mixture can be prepared up to 1 day in advance and refrigerated, tightly covered.

Ingredients

- ⅔ cup plain yogurt
- 1¾ pounds ground lamb
- 2 shallots, peeled and finely chopped
- 3 garlic cloves, peeled and minced
- ¼ cup chopped fresh parsley
- 2 tablespoons chopped fresh oregano or 2 teaspoons dried
- 1 tablespoon fresh thyme or 1 teaspoon dried
- 2 teaspoons ground cumin
- Salt and freshly ground black pepper to taste
- ½ cup finely chopped cucumber
- 2 ripe plum tomatoes, rinsed, cored, seeded, and finely chopped
- 4–6 (6-inch) pita breads

1¾ pounds ground pork

12 scallions, white parts and 2 inches of green tops, rinsed, trimmed, and thinly sliced, divided

¼ cup grated fresh ginger

¼ cup chopped fresh cilantro

4 garlic cloves, peeled and minced

¼ cup soy sauce

2 tablespoons dry sherry

½ cup finely chopped water chestnuts

Freshly ground black pepper to taste

½ cup Dijon mustard

¼ cup hoisin sauce*

4–6 sesame rolls, sliced in half

Lettuce, tomato slices, and thinly sliced onion

* Available in the Asian aisle of most supermarkets and in specialty markets.

Chinese Pork Burgers

Yield: 4–6 servings | Active time: 20 minutes | Start to finish: 45 minutes

1. Prepare a medium-hot grill according to the instructions given in Chapter 1.

2. Combine pork, half of the scallions, ginger, cilantro, garlic, soy sauce, sherry, water chestnuts, and pepper in a mixing bowl. Mix well and form into 4–6 (¾-inch-thick) burgers. Press with your thumb in the center of each burger to form an indentation; this keeps the burgers from creating a dome in the center. Combine mustard and hoisin sauce in a bowl, whisk well, and set aside.

3. Grill rolls cut-side down until toasted. Grill burgers beginning with the side with the indentation up, uncovered if using a charcoal grill, for a total time of 4–6 minutes per side or to an internal temperature of 150°F on an instant-read thermometer. Baste burgers with sauce for last 4 minutes of grilling.

4. Add remaining scallions to remaining sauce. Serve immediately on rolls with lettuce, tomato, and onion. Pass remaining basting sauce separately.

VARIATION: *Ground turkey or ground veal can be substituted for the pork. The turkey should be grilled to an internal temperature of 160°F or until cooked through and no longer pink.*

Note: The pork mixture can be prepared up to 1 day in advance and refrigerated, tightly covered.

Chinese Pork Burgers

Middle Eastern Lentil Burgers

Yield: 4–6 servings | Active time: 20 minutes | Start to finish: 40 minutes

1. Place lentils in a 2-quart saucepan, cover with water and add 1 teaspoon salt. Bring to a boil over medium-high heat, then reduce the heat to low and simmer lentils, covered, for 20 to 25 minutes or until cooked. Drain lentils, and place in a mixing bowl.

2. Prepare a medium-hot grill according to the instructions given in Chapter 1.

3. While lentils simmer, place pine nuts in a small dry skillet over medium heat. Toast nuts, shaking pan frequently, for 2–3 minutes, or until browned. Remove nuts from the pan, and set aside. Heat oil in the same small skillet over medium-high heat. Add onions and garlic, and cook, stirring frequently, for 3 minutes, or until onion is translucent. Add coriander and cumin, and cook, stirring constantly, for 1 minute. Add onion mixture to lentils, and stir well.

4. Puree ½ cup pine nuts and 1 cup lentil mixture in a food processor fitted with a metal blade. Scrape mixture back into a mixing bowl, and add remaining lentil mixture and remaining pine nuts. Season to taste with salt and pepper. Form mixture into 4–6 burgers that are ¾ inch thick.

5. Grill buns cut-side down until toasted. Grill burgers for 3 minutes per side, covered, turning them gently with a spatula. Serve immediately on buns with lettuce, tomato, and hummus.

Note: The lentil mixture can be prepared up to 1 day in advance and refrigerated, tightly covered. Allow it to reach room temperature before grilling the burgers.

2 cups lentils, picked over, rinsed, and drained

1 quart water

1 teaspoon salt

¾ cup pine nuts

2 tablespoons vegetable oil

1 medium onion, peeled and chopped

2 garlic cloves, peeled and minced

2 teaspoons ground coriander

1 teaspoon ground cumin

Salt and freshly ground black pepper to taste

6 sesame buns, sliced in half

Lettuce, tomato, and hummus

Chapter 11

Entree Salads

The recipes in this chapter can be considered a "two-fer." Entree salads—loaded with healthful fresh vegetables and some grilled protein—are also a great way to use up leftover grilled food from a previous meal. Stunning when they arrive at the table, the salads in this chapter are a complete meal, perhaps with the addition of some crusty bread. So do not be put off if the preparation time seems long; the salad is all you have to create.

1½ pounds boneless, skinless chicken breasts, rinsed and patted dry with paper towels

2 tablespoons freshly squeezed lime juice

2 tablespoons cider vinegar

1 tablespoon Dijon mustard

1 tablespoon honey

1 tablespoon chopped fresh parsley

2 teaspoons fresh thyme or ½ teaspoon dried

Salt and freshly ground black pepper to taste

½ cup olive oil

2 ripe peaches, peeled, stoned, and diced

½ small red onion, peeled and thinly sliced

6 cups mixed baby greens, rinsed and dried

Chicken and Peach Salad

Yield: 6–8 servings | Active time: 25 minutes | Start to finish: 35 minutes

1. Prepare a hot grill according to the instructions given in Chapter 1.

2. Trim chicken breasts of all visible fat, and pound to an even thickness of ½ inch between 2 sheets of plastic wrap. Place chicken breasts in a mixing bowl.

3. Combine lime juice, vinegar, mustard, honey, parsley, thyme, salt, and pepper in a jar with a tight-fitting lid, and shake well. Add olive oil, and shake well again.

4. Reserve half of dressing, then mix remaining dressing into bowl with chicken breasts.

5. Grill chicken for 2–3 minutes per side, uncovered, or until chicken is cooked through and no longer pink. Remove chicken from the grill, and cut into thin slices against the grain.

6. To serve, combine peaches, onion, and greens in a mixing bowl, and toss with enough dressing to coat lightly. Mound mixture onto a serving platter or individual plates, and top with chicken slices. Serve immediately, passing extra dressing separately.

Note: The dressing can be made up to 1 day in advance and refrigerated, tightly covered. Bring to room temperature before using.

Cajun Chicken Salad

Yield: 6–8 servings | Active time: 25 minutes | Start to finish: 35 minutes

1. Prepare a hot grill according to the instructions given in Chapter 1.

2. Trim chicken breasts of all visible fat, and pound to an even thickness of ½ inch between 2 sheets of plastic wrap. Place chicken breasts in a mixing bowl.

3. Combine olive oil, 2 garlic cloves, paprika, oregano, thyme, cayenne, salt, and pepper in a small bowl, and mix well. Pour mixture over chicken, and mix well to coat chicken.

4. Combine buttermilk, mayonnaise, vinegar, scallions, thyme, remaining garlic, salt, and pepper in a jar with a tight-fitting lid, and shake well. Set aside.

5. Grill chicken for 2–3 minutes per side, uncovered, or until chicken is cooked through and no longer pink. Remove chicken from the grill, and cut into thin slices against the grain.

6. To serve, combine lettuce, red pepper, onion, and tomatoes in a mixing bowl, and toss with enough dressing to coat lightly. Mound mixture onto a serving platter or individual plates, and top with chicken slices. Serve immediately, passing extra dressing separately.

VARIATION: *Grilled shrimp or cubes of salmon can be used instead of chicken for an aquatic treat.*

Note: The dressing can be made up to 1 day in advance and refrigerated, tightly covered. Bring to room temperature before using.

1½ pounds boneless, skinless chicken breasts, rinsed and patted dry with paper towels

¼ cup olive oil

4 garlic cloves, peeled and minced, divided

2 tablespoons paprika

1 tablespoon dried oregano

2 teaspoons dried thyme

½ teaspoon cayenne, or to taste

Salt and freshly ground black pepper to taste

½ cup buttermilk

½ cup mayonnaise

¼ cup distilled white vinegar

3 scallions, white parts and 2 inches of green tops, rinsed, trimmed, and chopped

1 tablespoon fresh thyme or 1 teaspoon dried

6–8 cups mixed baby greens, rinsed and dried

1 red bell pepper, seeds and ribs removed, and thinly sliced

½ small red onion, peeled and thinly sliced

1 pint cherry tomatoes, rinsed and halved

1½ pounds boneless,
  skinless chicken breasts,
  rinsed and patted dry
  with paper towels

1 large egg

1 (2-ounce) tube anchovy
  paste

5 garlic cloves, peeled and
  minced

¼ cup freshly squeezed
  lemon juice

2 tablespoons Dijon
  mustard

½ cup extra-virgin olive oil,
  divided

Freshly ground black
  pepper to taste

6–8 (½-inch-thick) slices
  French or Italian bread

6–8 cups baby greens or
  bite-sized pieces romaine
  lettuce, rinsed and dried

½ cup freshly grated
  Parmesan cheese

6–8 anchovy fillets
  (optional)

Grilled Chicken Caesar Salad

Yield: 6–8 servings | Active time: 25 minutes | Start to finish: 35 minutes

1. Prepare a hot grill according to the instructions given in Chapter 1.

2. Trim chicken breasts of all visible fat, and pound to an even thickness of ½ inch between 2 sheets of plastic wrap. Place chicken breasts in a mixing bowl.

3. To prepare dressing, bring a small saucepan of water to a boil over high heat. Add egg and boil for 1 minute. Remove egg from water with a slotted spoon and break it into a jar with a tight-fitting lid, scraping the inside of the shell. Add anchovy paste, garlic, lemon juice, and mustard, and shake well. Add ⅓ cup olive oil, and shake well again. Season to taste with pepper.

4. Reserve half of dressing, and mix remaining dressing into bowl with chicken breasts. Use reserved oil to brush both sides of bread.

5. Grill chicken for 2–3 minutes per side, uncovered, or until chicken is cooked through and no longer pink. Grill bread for 1–2 minutes per side, or until toasted. Remove chicken from the grill, and cut into thin slices against the grain. Remove bread from the grill, and cut into ½-inch croutons.

6. To serve, combine croutons, lettuce, and Parmesan in a mixing bowl, and toss with enough dressing to coat lightly. Mound mixture onto a serving platter or individual plates, and top with chicken slices and anchovies, if using. Serve immediately, passing extra dressing separately.

VARIATION: *Grilled shrimp or cubes of salmon can be used instead of chicken for an aquatic treat.*

Note: The dressing can be made up to 1 day in advance and refrigerated, tightly covered. Bring to room temperature before using.

Grilled Chicken Caesar Salad

2 (¾-pound) pork tenderloins, trimmed of fat and silver skin (method in Chapter 9)

Salt and freshly ground black pepper to taste

2 tablespoons chili powder

1 tablespoon ground cumin

1 teaspoon ground cinnamon

Pinch of ground allspice

¼ cup freshly squeezed orange juice

3 tablespoons freshly squeezed lime juice

1 tablespoon Dijon mustard

1 shallot, peeled and chopped

2 garlic cloves, peeled and minced

1 teaspoon curry powder

1 teaspoon fresh thyme or ¼ teaspoon dried

½ cup olive oil

3 navel oranges

⅓ pound baby spinach, rinsed and dried

1 head radicchio, rinsed, cored, and shredded

1 red bell pepper, seeds and ribs removed, and thinly sliced

4 scallions, white parts and 2 inches of green tops, rinsed, trimmed, and thinly sliced

2 ripe avocados, peeled and diced

Pork Salad with Citrus Vinaigrette

Yield: 6–8 servings | Active time: 25 minutes | Start to finish: 50 minutes

1. Prepare a dual-temperature hot-and-medium grill according to the instructions given in Chapter 1.

2. Rinse pork and pat dry with paper towels. Sprinkle pork with salt and pepper. Combine chili powder, cumin, cinnamon, and allspice in a small bowl. Rub mixture over pork, and set aside.

3. Combine orange juice, lime juice, mustard, shallot, garlic, curry powder, thyme, salt, and pepper in a jar with a tight-fitting lid, and shake well. Add olive oil, and shake well again. Set aside.

4. Prepare oranges: first cut away peel and the white pith below it. Then, to separate orange segments from internal membranes, slice down to the core on either side of each segment; set segments aside as you go.

5. Grill pork, uncovered if using a charcoal grill, on the hot side of the grill for 2–3 minutes per side, turning it in quarter turns, and then move pork to the cooler side of the grill. Grill for an additional 5–6 minutes per side for medium. Allow pork to rest for 5 minutes, then slice pork on the diagonal into ½-inch slices and set aside.

6. Combine oranges, spinach, radicchio, red pepper, scallions, and avocados in a large mixing bowl. Toss salad with ⅓ cup dressing. Mound mixture onto a serving platter or individual plates, and top with pork slices. Serve immediately, passing extra dressing separately.

Note: The dressing can be made up to 1 day in advance and refrigerated, tightly covered. Bring to room temperature before using.

Asian Steak Salad

Yield: 6–8 servings | Active time: 25 minutes | Start to finish: 4¼ hours, including 4 hours for marinating

1. Rinse steak and pat dry with paper towels. Score steak with a paring knife on both sides in a diagonal pattern ¼ inch deep.

2. Combine vinegar, soy sauce, mustard, hoisin sauce, ginger, garlic, scallions, and pepper in a jar with a tight-fitting lid, and shake well. Add vegetable and sesame oils, and shake well again.

3. Place steak in a heavy resealable plastic bag, and add ½ cup of dressing. Marinate steak, refrigerated, for 4 hours, turning the bag occasionally.

4. While steak marinates, place snow peas in a microwave-safe container with 1 tablespoon water. Microwave on high (100%) for 30 seconds. Plunge snow peas into a bowl of ice water. Drain. Combine snow peas with spinach, bean sprouts, cucumbers, and red pepper in a salad bowl, and refrigerate.

5. Prepare a hot grill according to the instructions given in Chapter 1.

6. Grill steak for 5–7 minutes, uncovered if using a charcoal grill, or until browned. Turn meat with tongs, and grill for an additional 2–3 minutes for medium rare, or to desired doneness. Allow steak to rest for 5 minutes, then slice it thinly against the grain on the diagonal.

6. To serve, toss salad with ⅓ cup of dressing. Mound mixture onto a serving platter or individual plates, and top with steak slices. Serve immediately, passing extra dressing separately.

VARIATION: *You can substitute slices of grilled chicken breast or fish steaks for the beef in this recipe. Consult a similar recipe for cooking instructions.*

Note: The dressing can be made up to 1 day in advance and refrigerated, tightly covered. Bring to room temperature before using.

---

1 (2-pound) flank steak

⅓ cup rice wine vinegar

3 tablespoons soy sauce

3 tablespoons Dijon mustard

2 tablespoons hoisin sauce*

3 tablespoons grated fresh ginger

4 garlic cloves, peeled and minced

2 scallions, trimmed and finely chopped

Freshly ground black pepper to taste

¾ cup vegetable oil

¼ cup Asian sesame oil*

¼ pound snow peas, tips removed

1 pound baby spinach leaves, rinsed and stemmed

¼ pound bean sprouts, rinsed

2 cucumbers, peeled, halved, and thinly sliced

1 red bell pepper, seeds and ribs removed, thinly sliced

* Available in the Asian aisle of most supermarkets and in specialty markets.

1½ pounds New York strip steak or boneless rib eye steak, at least 1 inch thick

Salt and freshly ground black pepper to taste

½ cup red wine vinegar

2 garlic cloves, peeled and minced

1 shallot, peeled and minced

2 tablespoons chopped fresh parsley

1 tablespoon fresh thyme or 1 teaspoon dried

2 teaspoons granulated sugar

1 cup olive oil

4 cups bite-sized pieces romaine lettuce, rinsed and dried

1 large head radicchio, rinsed, cored, and chopped

½ small red onion, peeled and thinly sliced

4 small tomatoes, rinsed, cored, and cut into wedges

1 cup crumbled blue cheese

Steak and Blue Cheese Salad

Yield: 4–6 servings | Active time: 25 minutes | Start to finish: 45 minutes

1. Prepare a dual-temperature hot-and-medium grill according to the instructions given in Chapter 1.

2. Sprinkle steaks with salt and pepper. Combine vinegar, garlic, shallot, parsley, thyme, sugar, salt, and pepper in a jar with a tight-fitting lid, and shake well. Add olive oil, and shake well again. Set aside.

3. Sear steaks on the hot side of the grill for 2–3 minutes per side, uncovered if using a charcoal grill, or until well browned. Transfer steaks to the cooler side of the grill, and cook for an additional 2–3 minutes per side for rare, when an instant-read thermometer registers 120°F. Remove steaks from the grill, and allow them to rest for 5 minutes.

4. Combine romaine, radicchio, onion, tomatoes, and blue cheese in a mixing bowl. To serve, toss salad with ⅓ cup of dressing. Mound mixture onto a serving platter or individual plates, and top with steak slices. Serve immediately, passing extra dressing separately.

Note: The dressing can be made up to 1 day in advance and refrigerated, tightly covered. Bring to room temperature before using.

Steak and Blue Cheese Salad

Middle Eastern Lamb Salad

Yield: 6–8 servings | Active time: 25 minutes | Start to finish: 1¼ hours

1 cup cracked-wheat bulgur

2 cups boiling water

1 (15-ounce) can garbanzo beans, drained and rinsed

2 large tomatoes, rinsed, cored, seeded, and diced

1 cup chopped fresh parsley

1 bunch scallions, white parts and 2 inches of green tops, rinsed, trimmed, and thinly sliced

½ cup freshly squeezed lemon juice

¼ cup chopped fresh mint

¼ cup olive oil

Salt and freshly ground black pepper to taste

1 (3-pound) butterflied boneless leg of lamb (method in Chapter 9)

3–4 (12-inch) metal skewers

½ head romaine lettuce, rinsed and dried

1. Place bulgur in a large mixing bowl. Stir in boiling water, cover the bowl, and allow bulgur to stand for 1 hour. Add beans, tomatoes, parsley, scallions, lemon juice, mint, olive oil, salt, and pepper to bulgur, and mix well. Refrigerate salad, tightly covered.

2. Prepare a hot grill according to the instructions given in Chapter 1. Preheat the oven to 375°F.

3. Sprinkle lamb with salt and pepper. Spear lamb lengthwise through the thickest part of the meat with the skewers to keep it level. Sear lamb on hot grill, uncovered, for 4 minutes per side.

4. Remove lamb from the grill, and place lamb in a broiler pan. Roast lamb for 15–20 minutes, or until it registers 125°F for medium-rare on an instant-read thermometer. Remove lamb from the oven, and cover it loosely with foil. Allow lamb to rest for 10 minutes, then carve into slices across the grain.

5. To serve, line a platter or individual plates with lettuce leaves, and mound bulgur salad on top of lettuce. Top salad with lamb slices, and serve immediately.

Note: The lamb can be seared up to 4 hours in advance and kept at room temperature before roasting. The bulgur salad can be made up to 1 day in advance and refrigerated, tightly covered.

8–12 (8-inch) bamboo skewers

⅓ cup freshly squeezed lemon juice

4 garlic cloves, peeled and minced

2 tablespoons chopped fresh oregano or 2 teaspoons dried

2 tablespoons chopped fresh parsley

Salt and freshly ground black pepper to taste

½ cup extra-virgin olive oil, divided

1 pint cherry tomatoes, rinsed and halved

½ English cucumber, cut into ⅓-inch dice

½ small red onion, peeled, halved lengthwise, and thinly sliced

1½ pounds extra-large (16–20 per pound) raw shrimp, peeled and deveined

1 orange or yellow bell pepper, seeds and ribs removed, and cut into ½-inch slices

4–6 cups baby spinach, rinsed and dried

1 cup crumbled feta cheese

1 cup pitted kalamata olives, sliced

Greek Shrimp Salad

Yield: 4–6 servings | Active time: 20 minutes | Start to finish: 40 minutes

1. Soak bamboo skewers in warm water to cover, and prepare a medium-hot grill according to the instructions given in Chapter 1.

2. Combine lemon juice, garlic, oregano, parsley, salt, and pepper in a jar with a tight-fitting lid, and shake well. Add ⅓ cup olive oil, and shake well again.

3. Place tomatoes, cucumbers, and red onion in a large mixing bowl. Toss with one-third of dressing, and refrigerate. Place shrimp in a heavy resealable plastic bag, and add one-third of dressing. Seal and turn bag to coat shrimp evenly. Marinate shrimp at room temperature for 10 minutes, or up to 30 minutes refrigerated.

4. Grill pepper slices, covered, for 3–5 minutes, or until soft. Remove peppers from the grill, and slice into strips. Add peppers to bowl with other vegetables.

Greek Shrimp Salad

5. Remove shrimp from marinade, and discard marinade. Divide shrimp into 4–6 groups, and thread each group onto 2 parallel skewers. Grill shrimp, covered, for 2 minutes per side, or until pink and cooked through. Remove shrimp from skewers.

6. To serve, place 1 portion lettuce on each plate, and top with vegetables and shrimp. Sprinkle feta and olives on top, and serve immediately, passing remaining dressing separately.

VARIATION: *Any firm white-fleshed fish fillet such as halibut or cod will be just as delicious as the shrimp and will cook in the same amount of time. You can also substitute ¾-inch cubes of boneless, skinless chicken breast. The chicken should be marinated refrigerated for 1 hour, and the pieces should be cooked for 4–6 minutes per side, or until cooked through and no longer pink.*

Note: The dressing can be made up to 1 day in advance and refrigerated, tightly covered. Bring to room temperature before using.

Tuna Salad Niçoise

Yield: 4–6 servings | Active time: 20 minutes | Start to finish: 45 minutes

1. Place potatoes in a saucepan of salted water, and bring to a boil over high heat. Boil potatoes for 8–10 minutes, or until tender. Add green beans, and boil 2 minutes more. Drain vegetables, and rinse under cold running water. Refrigerate vegetables until cold.

2. Prepare a hot grill according to the instructions given in Chapter 1. Sprinkle tuna with salt and pepper, and place it on a sheet of plastic wrap in the freezer for 20–30 minutes.

3. Combine lemon juice, mustard, herbes de Provence, salt, and pepper in a jar with a tight-fitting lid, and shake well. Add olive oil, and shake well again.

4. Grill tuna steaks, uncovered if using a charcoal grill, for 2–3 minutes per side; the inside should remain almost raw, or cook to desired doneness. Slice steaks into ¼-inch slices against the grain, and set aside.

5. Toss salad greens with one-quarter of dressing, and arrange on a platter or individual plates. Top greens with tuna, potatoes, and green beans, and drizzle with additional dressing. Scatter olives, tomatoes, capers, parsley, and Parmesan over all, and serve immediately, passing remaining dressing separately.

Note: The vegetables can be boiled and the dressing can be made up to 1 day in advance and refrigerated, tightly covered. Bring the dressing to room temperature before using.

1 pound baby new potatoes, scrubbed and quartered

¼ pound green beans, rinsed and stemmed

3 (8-ounce) fresh tuna steaks, at least ¾ inch thick

Salt and freshly ground black pepper to taste

¼ cup freshly squeezed lemon juice

2 teaspoons Dijon mustard

1 teaspoon herbes de Provence

⅓ cup extra-virgin olive oil

4–6 cups mixed baby greens, rinsed and dried

½ cup pitted Niçoise or other oil-cured black olives, halved lengthwise

1 cup cherry tomatoes, rinsed and halved

2 tablespoons capers, drained and rinsed

¼ cup chopped fresh parsley leaves

¼ cup freshly grated Parmesan cheese

Chapter 12

Combination Cooking

This chapter is not one you will find in many cookbooks on grilling; it is the result of literally decades of experimentation as I have tried to push the limits of what can be cooked on a grill and how to give food the best flavor. All of the recipes in this chapter start on the grill; they are then finished in a conventional oven. Some recipes are then roasted in a relatively cool oven to complete cooking, while others begin by being seared or smoked on the grill and are then braised to that wonderful term, fork tender. The chapter begins with charts on how to time foods cooked by these methods.

Timing Rolled Roasts

Roasts cook more evenly if they are boned and rolled rather than left on the bone. While bones help retain moisture, the meat next to bones does not cook at the same rate since the bones act as insulation against the air carrying the heat. When tied, the string should be firm enough to hold the meat together in a neat cylinder, but should not be so tight as to be pressing into the flesh so that the exterior of the roast is bumpy. When the tissue is compressed at the points where the strings are tied, those portions of meat will cook at a slower rate, so the interior will not be evenly cooked.

Here is a chart of the general temperatures to which meats are roasted:

Roasting Temperature for Meat	
MEAT	**DESIRED INTERNAL TEMPERATURE**
Beef and Lamb	120°F—Rare 125°F–130°F—Medium Rare 135°F—Medium
Pork	145°F–150°F
Veal	150°F–155°F

While most cookbooks calculate roasting times in an equation of minutes per pound, I have a different method. I roast meats by the circumference. A 3-pound boneless pork loin can be short and squat, or it can be long and thin.

The easiest way to determine the circumference of a roast is with a tape measure. Stand the roast on its end, and place the tape measure snugly around what would be the waistline. Here is a chart to help you judge when to start taking the temperature of different roasts:

ROASTING TIMES FOR MEATS

These are total times for boneless roasts, with the initial searing taking place on the grill, and then the meat roasted in a 350°F oven for the remainder of the cooking time.

Roasting Times for Meats			
CIRCUMFERENCE	BEEF/LAMB (125°F)	VEAL (150°F)	PORK (150°F)
9 inches	30–35 min.	50–55 min.	55–60 min.
10 inches	35–45 min.	55–65 min.	60–70 min.
11 inches	45–50 min.	65–70 min.	75–85 min.
12 inches	55–60 min.	70–75 min.	85–95 min.
13 inches	60–65 min.	75–85 min.	95–105 min.
14 inches	70–75 min.	85–95 min.	105–115 min.
15 inches	75–80 min.	95–110 min.	115–125 min.
16 inches	80–90 min.	110–115 min.	125–130 min.

Great Year-Round Grilling in the Southeast

Simplified North Carolina Pulled Pork Barbecue

1 (6–8-pound) boneless Boston pork butt

¼ cup vegetable oil

4 garlic cloves, peeled and minced

1 small onion, peeled and chopped

2 tablespoons paprika

2 tablespoons firmly packed light brown sugar

1 tablespoon dry mustard

Salt and freshly ground black pepper to taste

3 cups hickory chips

3 cups chicken stock or pork stock

North Carolina Barbecue Sauce (recipe on page 17)

10–12 hamburger buns

2–3 cups coleslaw

Yield: 10–12 servings | Active time: 20 minutes | Start to finish: 9 hours, including 6 hours for marinating

1. Rinse pork and pat dry with paper towels. Combine vegetable oil, garlic, onion, paprika, sugar, mustard, salt, and pepper in a small bowl. Rub paste all over pork, and refrigerate pork for a minimum of 6 hours or up to 24 hours, tightly covered with plastic wrap.

2. Prepare a medium-hot grill according to the instructions given in Chapter 1. If using a charcoal grill, soak hickory chips in water for 30 minutes. If using a gas grill, create a packet for wood chips as described in Chapter 1.

3. Preheat the oven to 350°F. Place wood chips on the grill. Sear pork, covered, for a total of 25 minutes, turning with tongs after 10 minutes. Remove pork from the grill, and cut into 3-inch cubes.

4. Transfer pork cubes to a roasting pan, and add stock. Bring to a boil on top of the stove, then transfer to the oven, and bake for 2–2½ hours, covered, or until fork tender.

5. Using 2 forks, shred pork into bite-sized pieces. Mix meat with North Carolina Barbecue Sauce. To serve, mound meat onto buns, and top with coleslaw. Serve immediately.

Note: The meat can be prepared up to 3 days in advance and refrigerated, tightly covered. Reheat, covered with foil, in a 350°F oven for 20–30 minutes, or until hot.

Smoked Beef Brisket with Barbecue Sauce

2 cups hickory or mesquite chips

1 (3–4-pound) beef brisket

2 garlic cloves, peeled and crushed

Salt and freshly ground black pepper to taste

2 cups beef stock

1 cup My Favorite Barbecue Sauce (recipe on page 18) or commercial barbecue sauce, heated

Yield: 8–10 servings | Active time: 20 minutes | Start to finish: 3½ hours

1. Prepare a medium-hot grill according to the instructions given in Chapter 1. If using a charcoal grill, soak hickory or mesquite chips in water for 30 minutes. If using a gas grill, create a packet for wood chips as described in Chapter 1.

2. Rinse brisket and pat dry with paper towels. Rub brisket with garlic, and season to taste with salt and pepper.

3. Preheat the oven to 350°F. Place wood chips on the grill. Sear brisket, covered, for a total of 20 minutes, turning with tongs after 10 minutes.

4. Transfer brisket to a roasting pan, and add stock. Bring to a boil on top of the stove, then transfer to the oven, and bake for 2–2½ hours, covered, or until fork tender.

5. Remove brisket to a warm platter and tip the roasting pan to spoon off as much grease as possible. Slice brisket against the grain into thin slices. Spoon some pan juices over meat, and pass barbecue sauce separately.

VARIATION: *You can also use this recipe for a boneless pork shoulder; the cooking time will be reduced to 1½–2 hours.*

Note: The brisket can be prepared up to 2 days in advance and refrigerated. If cooked in advance, remove the layer of grease, which will have hardened on the top. Reheat, covered, in a 350°F oven for 25–35 minutes, or until hot.

Leg of Lamb with Garlic, Rosemary, and Lemon
Yield: 6–8 servings | Active time: 20 minutes | Start to finish: 1½ hours

½ leg of lamb, boned, rolled, and tied, to yield 3 pounds meat
1 cup mesquite chips
10 garlic cloves, peeled
Zest of 1 lemon, cut into thin strips
3 sprigs fresh rosemary, leaves removed
1 tablespoon kosher salt
1 teaspoon freshly ground black pepper
½ cup beef stock

1. Allow meat to reach room temperature and cut deep slits into any thick portions with a paring knife.

2. Prepare a hot grill according to the instructions given in Chapter 1. If using a charcoal grill, soak mesquite chips in water for 30 minutes. If using a gas grill, create a packet for wood chips as described in Chapter 1.

3. Combine garlic, lemon zest, and rosemary leaves in a food processor fitted with a steel blade and chop finely using an on-and-off pulsing action. Scrape mixture into a small bowl and stir in salt and pepper. Stuff garlic mixture into all the crevices of the meat formed when it was boned, as well as into the slits. Rub some of mixture all over exterior of roast.

4. Preheat the oven to 350°F. Place mesquite chips on the grill. Sear lamb for a total of 10 minutes, covered, turning with tongs to sear all sides. Remove lamb from the grill and place in a roasting pan.

5. Roast lamb, uncovered, for 45–60 minutes, or until the temperature registers 125°F on an instant-read thermometer. The roasting time will depend on the thickness of the roll; consult the chart at the beginning of this chapter. Remove lamb from the oven and place it on a platter loosely covered with aluminum foil. Allow lamb to rest for 15 minutes to allow juices to be reabsorbed into meat.

6. Pour grease out of the roasting pan and pour in stock. Place the pan over medium-high heat and stir often to dislodge any brown bits clinging to the bottom of the pan. Carve the meat into slices, adding any juices to the pan, and pass sauce separately.

Note: The roast can be seared up to 3 hours in advance of roasting it; keep it at room temperature, lightly covered.

1 cup mesquite chips

6 (1-pound) lamb shanks

Salt and freshly ground
black pepper to taste

⅓ cup olive oil

2 medium onions, peeled
and diced

2 celery ribs, rinsed,
trimmed, and diced

2 carrots, peeled, trimmed,
and sliced

4 garlic cloves, peeled and
minced

2 tablespoons chopped
fresh parsley

1 tablespoon chopped
fresh rosemary or 1
teaspoon dried

1 tablespoon chopped
fresh oregano or 1
teaspoon dried

2 teaspoons fresh thyme or
½ teaspoon dried

2 tablespoons tomato
paste

1½ cups Barolo, or other
dry red wine

1 cup beef stock

1 tablespoon cornstarch

2 tablespoons cold water

Braised Lamb Shanks

Yield: 6 servings | Active time: 20 minutes | Start to finish: 3 hours

1. Prepare a medium-hot grill according to the instructions given in Chapter 1. If using a charcoal grill, soak mesquite chips in water for 30 minutes. If using a gas grill, create a packet for wood chips as described in Chapter 1.

2. Wipe lamb shanks well with a damp cloth and remove any fat. Season with salt and pepper, and set aside.

3. While grill heats, heat oil in a Dutch oven over medium-high heat. Add onions, celery, carrots, and garlic, and cook, stirring frequently, for 3 minutes, or until onions are translucent.

4. Preheat the oven to 350°F. Place mesquite chips on the grill. Sear lamb shanks for a total of 15 minutes, covered, turning shanks with tongs to sear all sides.

5. Transfer shanks to the Dutch oven, and add parsley, rosemary, oregano, thyme, tomato paste, wine, and stock. Bring to a boil on top of the stove, then transfer to the oven, and bake for 1½–2 hours, or until fork tender.

6. Remove shanks to a warm platter and tip the Dutch oven to spoon off as much grease as possible. Cook sauce over medium heat until reduced by half. Mix cornstarch and water in a small cup, and add to sauce. Simmer for 3 minutes or until slightly thickened. Season sauce to taste with salt and pepper, then pour sauce over shanks, and serve immediately.

Note: The shanks can be prepared up to 3 days in advance and refrigerated. If cooked in advance, remove the layer of grease, which will have hardened on the top. Reheat, covered, in a 350°F oven for 25–35 minutes, or until hot.

Braised Lamb Shanks

2 cups hickory or apple wood chips

1 (3-pound) boneless center cut pork loin roast

5 garlic cloves, peeled and minced, divided

2 tablespoons dried sage

1 tablespoon dried thyme

½ teaspoon ground allspice

Salt and freshly ground black pepper to taste

3 large tomatoes, cut in half

1 large onion, cut in half

1 Granny Smith apple, peeled, cored, and quartered

½ cup granulated sugar

½ cup cider vinegar

¼ cup golden raisins

2 tablespoons grated fresh ginger

¼ teaspoon cayenne

Pork Loin with Smoked Apple Chutney

Yield: 6–8 servings | Active time: 25 minutes | Start to finish: 1¾ hours

1. Prepare a hot grill according to the instructions given in Chapter 1. If using a charcoal grill, soak hickory or apple wood chips in water for 30 minutes. If using a gas grill, create a packet for wood chips as described in Chapter 1.

2. Rinse pork and pat dry with paper towels. Combine 3 garlic cloves, sage, thyme, allspice, salt, and pepper in a small bowl. Rub mixture into surfaces of pork.

3. Preheat the oven to 350°F. Place wood chips on the grill. Sear pork for a total of 10 minutes, covered, turning with tongs to sear all sides. Remove pork from the grill and place in a roasting pan.

4. Roast pork, uncovered, for 45–60 minutes, or until the temperature registers 145°F on an instant-read thermometer. The roasting time will depend on the thickness of the meat; consult the chart at the beginning of this chapter.

5. While pork roasts, prepare chutney. Cover the grill with a small-holed fish grill and place tomatoes, onion, and apple on the grill. Cover the grill with a lid and smoke vegetables and apple for 10 minutes. Remove vegetables and apple from the grill. Peel, core, and seed tomatoes. Peel and finely dice onion, and apples. Place them in a large saucepan and add remaining garlic, sugar, vinegar, raisins, ginger, and cayenne.

6. Bring chutney to a boil over medium heat. Simmer, uncovered, for 30 minutes, or until thick, stirring occasionally.

7. Remove pork from the oven and place it on a platter loosely covered with aluminum foil. Allow pork to rest for 15 minutes to allow juices to be reabsorbed into meat. Then slice thinly against the grain. Serve immediately, and pass chutney separately.

Note: The roast can be seared up to 3 hours in advance of roasting it; keep it at room temperature, lightly covered.

Aromatic Roast Chicken

Serves: 4 | Active time: 15 minutes | Start to finish: 2 hours

1. Prepare a medium-hot grill according to the instructions given in Chapter 1. If using a charcoal grill, soak wood chips in water for 30 minutes. If using a gas grill, create a packet for wood chips as described in Chapter 1.

2. Rinse chicken, and pat dry with paper towels. Place 2 sprigs each of parsley and rosemary, 3 garlic cloves, and orange quarters in cavity of chicken. Sprinkle salt and pepper inside cavity, and close cavity with skewers.

3. Chop remaining parsley, rosemary, and garlic, and mix with butter. Season to taste with salt and pepper. Gently stuff mixture under skin of breast meat. Rub skin with salt and pepper. Truss chicken, if desired.

4. Preheat the oven to 350°F. Place wood chips on the grill. Sear chicken for a total of 15 minutes, covered, turning with tongs to brown all sides. Remove chicken from the grill, and place in a roasting pan, breast-side up.

5. Add onion, carrot, celery, and ½ cup chicken stock to the roasting pan. Cook an additional 1–1¼ hours, or until the juices run clear and the temperature of the dark meat registers 180°F on an instant-read thermometer. Remove chicken from the oven, and allow it to rest for 10 minutes, lightly covered.

6. Spoon all grease out of the pan, and add remaining chicken stock to the pan. Stir over medium-high heat until liquid is reduced to a syrupy consistency. Strain sauce into a sauce boat, and add to it any liquid that accumulates on the platter when chicken is carved. Carve chicken, and serve immediately.

VARIATION: *Tarragon can be substituted for the rosemary and parsley, and white wine can be used instead of chicken stock.*

Note: The chicken can be prepared for searing and roasting up to 6 hours in advance and refrigerated, tightly covered.

1 cup mesquite, hickory, or apple wood chips

1 (3½–4-pound) whole chicken, giblets removed

4 sprigs fresh parsley, divided

4 sprigs fresh rosemary, divided

6 garlic cloves, peeled, divided

1 orange, quartered

Salt and freshly ground black pepper to taste

4 tablespoons (½ stick) unsalted butter, softened

1 small onion, peeled and roughly chopped

1 carrot, peeled and thickly sliced

1 celery rib, rinsed, trimmed, and roughly chopped

1½ cups chicken stock, divided

Aromatic Roast Chicken

Chapter 13

Pizzas

Cooking thin-crust pizzas on the grill is now all the rage, and they can be topped with myriad ingredients. The key to a successful grilled pizza is that they must be small; it is impossible to flip a large round on the grill, and it is essential to grill both sides of the dough. I usually make pizzas in two batches, and cut up the first batch to allow diners to start munching while the second batch cooks. If your grill is large enough to accommodate all four circles at once, go ahead and cook them simultaneously.

For an easy alternative to making pizza dough, in almost all cities you can now purchase ready-to-bake balls of pizza dough in the refrigerated dairy case. With a few balls of pizza dough handy, any pizza can be on the table in less time than it takes to have one delivered!

3 cups all-purpose flour, plus extra for working dough

1 package dry or fresh active yeast

1 teaspoon salt

1 tablespoon honey

2 tablespoons olive oil

¾ cup water

Basic Pizza Dough and Procedure

Yield: 4 (8-inch) pizzas | Active time: 15 minutes | Start to finish: 50 minutes, including 30 minutes for rising

1. Place flour and yeast in a mixing bowl or the bowl of an electric mixer fitted with a dough hook. Add salt, honey, olive oil, and water. Mix well until the dough forms a soft ball.

2. Transfer dough to a lightly floured surface and knead for 5 minutes or until smooth. Place dough in a greased deep mixing bowl and allow dough to rest, covered with a clean dry towel, for 30 minutes.

3. Divide dough into 4 equal parts, and roll each piece into a smooth, tight ball. Place balls on a flat dish, covered with a damp towel, and refrigerate until grilling time. (This can be done up to 6 hours in advance, but dough should be removed from the refrigerator 1 hour before grilling to reach room temperature.)

4. Lightly flour a work surface, and using the fleshy part of your fingertips, flatten each dough ball into a circle approximately 6 inches in diameter, leaving outer edge thicker than center. Dust dough on both sides with flour. Lift dough from the work surface and gently stretch the edges, working clockwise, to form dough circles that are ¼ inch thick. Sprinkle additional flour on pizza paddles or baking sheets, and place pizza circles on top of flour. Lightly rub a long sheet of plastic wrap with flour, then invert loosely over pizza rounds and let them stand to puff slightly while preparing the grill, 10 to 20 minutes.

VARIATIONS: *Feel free to add a few tablespoons of chopped fresh herbs to the basic pizza dough.*

Provençal Vegetable Pizza
Yield: 4 servings | Active time: 20 minutes | Start to finish: 35 minutes

- 2 medium yellow squash, trimmed and cut into ¼-inch slices
- 2 Italian eggplant, trimmed and cut into ¼-inch slices
- 1 red bell pepper, seeds and ribs removed, and quartered lengthwise
- ½ cup extra-virgin olive oil, divided
- Salt and freshly ground black pepper to taste
- ¾ cup black olive tapenade, homemade or purchased
- 3 tablespoons chopped fresh oregano or 1 tablespoon dried
- 2 tablespoons chopped fresh parsley
- 1 tablespoon fresh thyme or 1 teaspoon dried
- 2 cups grated Gruyère cheese
- 2 (10-inch) aluminum pie tins

1. Prepare a medium-hot grill according to the instructions given in Chapter 1. Shape pizza dough into 4 individual ¼-inch-thick rounds as described above in the recipe for Basic Pizza Dough.

2. Brush squash, eggplant, and pepper slices with olive oil, and sprinkle with salt and pepper. Grill squash and eggplant for 2 minutes per side, covered, or until tender. Grill pepper slices for 5 minutes per side, covered, or until tender. When cool enough to handle, slice peppers into thin strips. Combine tapenade, oregano, parsley, and thyme in a small bowl, and stir well. Set aside.

3. Brush dough rounds with olive oil, and sprinkle with salt and pepper. Gently flip 2 dough rounds onto the grill, oiled-side down. Grill, uncovered, for 1½–2 minutes, or until grill marks form; burst bubbles that may appear on the surface with a long-handled meat fork. Brush tops with olive oil, and invert pizzas onto a baking sheet with the grilled side up.

3. Spread crusts with tapenade mixture, stopping ½ inch from the edge. Divide vegetables on top of tapenade, and then sprinkle each pizza with ½ cup cheese.

4. Return pizzas to the grill, and cover with pie tins. Grill, covered, for 1½–2 minutes, or until browned and cheese has melted. Serve immediately, and repeat with remaining 2 pizza rounds.

Note: The vegetables can be grilled up to 1 day in advance and refrigerated, tightly covered. Allow them to reach room temperature before using.

1 recipe Basic Pizza Dough or purchased pizza dough

8 ripe plum tomatoes, rinsed, cored, seeded, and chopped

¼ cup extra-virgin olive oil, divided

Salt and freshly ground black pepper to taste

½ pound whole-milk mozzarella cheese, thinly sliced

½ cup firmly packed shredded fresh basil leaves

¼ cup freshly grated Parmesan cheese

2 (10-inch) aluminum pie tins

Pizza Margherita

Yield: 4 servings | Active time: 20 minutes | Start to finish: 30 minutes

1. Prepare a medium-hot grill according to the instructions given in Chapter 1. Shape pizza dough into 4 individual ¼-inch-thick rounds as described above in the recipe for Basic Pizza Dough.

2. Place tomatoes in a sieve set over a mixing bowl to drain. Brush dough rounds with olive oil, and sprinkle with salt and pepper. Gently flip 2 dough rounds onto the grill, oiled-side down. Grill, uncovered, for 1½–2 minutes, or until grill marks form; burst bubbles that may appear on the surface with a long-handled meat fork. Brush tops with olive oil, and invert pizzas onto a baking sheet with the grilled side up.

3. Cover crusts with mozzarella and Parmesan, and then tomatoes, stopping ½ inch from the edge. Scatter basil over the top. Season to taste with salt and pepper, and drizzle with more olive oil.

4. Return pizzas to the grill, and cover with pie tins. Grill, covered, for 1½–2 minutes, or until browned and cheese has melted. Serve immediately, and repeat with remaining 2 pizza rounds.

VARIATION: *While it would not be authentic, either fresh oregano or fresh chopped rosemary can be substituted for the basil.*

Pizza Margherita

Prosciutto Pizza

Yield: 4 servings | Active time: 15 minutes | Start to finish: 35 minutes

1. Prepare a medium-hot grill according to the instructions given in Chapter 1. Shape pizza dough into 4 individual ¼-inch-thick rounds as described above in the recipe for Basic Pizza Dough.

2. Heat ¼ cup olive oil in a large skillet over medium-high heat. Add red bell peppers and cook, stirring frequently, for 5 minutes or until peppers are soft. Mix remaining ¼ cup oil with crushed red pepper, and set aside. Combine mozzarella and fontina cheeses, and set aside.

3. Brush dough rounds with seasoned olive oil, and sprinkle with salt and pepper. Gently flip 2 dough rounds onto the grill, oiled-side down. Grill, uncovered, for 1½–2 minutes, or until grill marks form; burst bubbles that may appear on the surface with a long-handled meat fork. Brush tops with olive oil, and invert pizzas onto a baking sheet with the grilled side up.

4. Spread mixed cheeses on top, reserving 1 cup cheese, stopping ½-inch from the edge. Sprinkle with basil, top with tomatoes, prosciutto, red peppers, and scallions. Dot with goat cheese, and finish by sprinkling with reserved cheese.

5. Return pizzas to the grill, and cover with pie tins. Grill, covered, for 1½–2 minutes, or until browned and cheese has melted. Serve immediately, and repeat with remaining 2 pizza rounds.

1 recipe Basic Pizza Dough or purchased pizza dough

½ cup olive oil, divided

2 red bell peppers, seeds and ribs removed, and thinly sliced

1 tablespoon crushed red pepper flakes

¾ pound fresh whole-milk mozzarella cheese, grated

¼ pound fontina cheese, grated

Salt and freshly ground black pepper to taste

½ cup chopped fresh basil

4 ripe plum tomatoes, rinsed, cored, seeded, and thinly sliced

6 ounces prosciutto, cut into fine julienne strips

4 scallions, white parts and 2 inches of green tops, rinsed, trimmed, and thinly sliced

4 ounces fresh goat cheese, crumbled

2 (10-inch) aluminum pie tins

1 recipe Basic Pizza Dough
   or purchased pizza dough

¼ pound smoked bacon

¼ cup extra-virgin olive oil

Salt and freshly ground
   pepper to taste

3 cups grated cheddar
   cheese

4 ripe plum tomatoes,
   rinsed, cored, seeded, and
   thinly sliced

1 cup sliced mushrooms

2 (10-inch) aluminum pie
   tins

Bacon, Tomato, Mushroom, and Cheddar Pizza

Yield: 4 servings | Active time: 15 minutes | Start to finish: 35 minutes

1. Prepare a medium-hot grill according to the instructions given in Chapter 1. Shape pizza dough into 4 individual ¼-inch-thick rounds as described above in the recipe for Basic Pizza Dough.

2. Place bacon slices in a heavy skillet, and cook over medium-high heat, turning pieces as necessary, until bacon is crisp. Remove bacon with tongs, and drain on paper towels. When cool, crumble bacon, and set aside.

3. Brush dough rounds with olive oil, and sprinkle with salt and pepper. Gently flip 2 dough rounds onto the grill, oiled-side down. Grill, uncovered, for 1½–2 minutes, or until grill marks form; burst bubbles that may appear on the surface with a long-handled meat fork. Brush tops with olive oil, and invert pizzas onto a baking sheet with the grilled side up.

4. Cover crusts with cheddar, then tomatoes and mushrooms, stopping ½ inch from the edge. Scatter bacon over the top. Season to taste with salt and pepper.

5. Return pizzas to the grill, and cover with pie tins. Grill, covered, for 1½–2 minutes, or until browned and cheese has melted. Serve immediately, and repeat with remaining 2 pizza rounds.

Bacon, Tomato, Mushroom, and Cheddar Pizza

Greek-Style Pita Pizzas

Yield: 4 servings | Active time: 10 minutes | Start to finish: 35 minutes

1. Prepare a medium-hot grill according to the instructions given in Chapter 1. Combine tomatoes, olives, onion, 2 tablespoons olive oil, oregano, salt, and pepper in a mixing bowl. Mix well.

2. Brush pita breads with olive oil, and sprinkle with salt and pepper. Gently flip 2 pita breads onto the grill, oiled-side down. Grill, uncovered, for 1½–2 minutes, or until grill marks form. Brush tops with olive oil, and invert pitas onto a baking sheet with the grilled side up.

3. Cover crusts with vegetable mixture, stopping ½ inch from the edge. Scatter feta over the top. Season to taste with salt and pepper.

4. Return pizzas to the grill, and cover with pie tins. Grill, covered, for 1½–2 minutes, or until browned and cheese has melted. Repeat with remaining 2 pita breads. Serve immediately.

4 ripe plum tomatoes, rinsed, cored, seeded, and diced

½ cup chopped pitted kalamata olives

¼ cup chopped red onion

4 tablespoons olive oil, divided

2 tablespoons chopped fresh oregano or 2 teaspoons dried

Salt and freshly ground black pepper to taste

4 (8-inch) whole-wheat pita breads

½ cup crumbled feta cheese

2 (10-inch) aluminum pie tins

Chapter 14

Vegetables

It is only in recent decades that Americans have come to appreciate the wonderful flavors and textures that result from grilling vegetables. Cooking vegetables over high heat evaporates some of the high water content and, therefore, intensifies the natural, sweet flavor.

Grilling accentuates vegetables' natural sugars.

Mixed Vegetable Kebabs

Yield: 4–6 servings | Active time: 20 minutes | Start to finish: 45 minutes

1. Soak bamboo skewers in warm water to cover, and prepare a medium-hot grill according to the instructions given in Chapter 1.

2. Mix garlic with oil, and set aside. Cut onion in half horizontally, and then cut halves into 8 wedges each. Cut bell peppers into 1½-inch squares. Cut eggplant into 1½-inch cubes. Cut zucchini into 1½-inch segments. Cut mushroom caps into eighths.

3. Rub all vegetables with garlic oil, and sprinkle with salt and pepper.

4. Thread vegetables alternately onto 2 parallel skewers. Grill kebabs, covered, giving them quarter turns every 2½–3 minutes, for a total of 10–12 minutes, or until vegetables are tender. Remove kebabs from the grill, and serve immediately.

Note: The kebabs can be prepared for grilling up to 6 hours in advance and kept at room temperature.

- 8–12 (8-inch) bamboo skewers
- 3 garlic cloves, peeled and minced
- ¼ cup olive oil
- 1 red onion, peeled
- 2 orange or yellow bell peppers, seeds and ribs removed, and halved
- 1 Italian eggplant
- 2 small zucchini, rinsed and trimmed
- 2 portobello mushroom caps, stemmed, and wiped with a damp paper towel
- Salt and freshly ground black pepper to taste

Grilled Asparagus

Yield: 4–6 servings | Active time: 10 minutes | Start to finish: 30 minutes

1. Soak bamboo skewers in warm water to cover, and prepare a medium-hot grill according to the instructions given in Chapter 1.

2. Break off woody ends from asparagus, and soak asparagus in water to cover for 10 minutes, rubbing tips to dislodge any lingering grit.

3. Divide asparagus into groups, and thread them horizontally with 2 skewers per bunch into loose groups; do not push them together too tightly. Brush asparagus with oil, and sprinkle with salt and pepper.

4. Grill asparagus, covered, for 3–4 minutes per side, turning bunches with tongs. Serve immediately.

- 10 (8-inch) bamboo skewers
- 2 pounds medium asparagus
- 3 tablespoons olive oil
- Salt and freshly ground black pepper to taste

4–6 ears fresh corn

Kitchen twine

3 tablespoons unsalted butter, melted

Salt and freshly ground black pepper to taste

Grilled Corn

Yield: 4–6 servings | Active time: 10 minutes | Start to finish: 35 minutes

1. Prepare a medium-hot grill according to the instructions given in Chapter 1.

2. Break stem end off corn, and discard all but 1 layer of husks. Pull back remaining husks, and pull off as much corn silk as possible. Draw husks back over kernels, and tie husks with kitchen twine. Soak corn in cold water to cover for 10 minutes.

3. Grill corn, uncovered if using a charcoal grill, for a total of 8–10 minutes, turning it with tongs every 1½–2 minutes. Corn is done when husks are charred and outline of kernels is visible.

4. Remove corn from the grill, and when cool enough to handle, remove and discard husks and any remaining corn silks. To serve, brush corn with melted butter, and season with salt and pepper to taste. Serve immediately.

Grilled Corn

Rosemary Potatoes

Yield: 4–6 servings | Active time: 20 minutes | Start to finish: 1 hour

8–12 (8-inch) bamboo skewers

1½ pounds baby potatoes, no more than 2 inches in diameter, scrubbed and halved

⅓ cup olive oil

3 tablespoons finely chopped fresh rosemary

Salt and freshly ground black pepper to taste

1. Soak bamboo skewers in warm water to cover, and prepare a medium-hot grill according to the instructions given in Chapter 1.

2. Place potatoes in a saucepan, and cover with cold water. Salt water, and bring potatoes to a boil over high heat. Reduce the heat to medium-high, and boil potatoes for 10–12 minutes, or until just tender. Drain potatoes, and toss them with ¼ cup olive oil, rosemary, salt, and pepper.

3. Thread potatoes onto 2 parallel skewers. Grill potatoes, uncovered if using a charcoal grill, for a total of 4–5 minutes, turning them with tongs occasionally, or until grill marks appear. Remove skewers from the grill, and drizzle with remaining olive oil. Serve immediately.

VARIATION: *In place of rosemary, try fresh oregano or basil in this recipe, and you can add a few crushed garlic cloves to the oil, too.*

Herbed Zucchini

Yield: 4–6 servings | Active time: 15 minutes | Start to finish: 35 minutes

4–6 small zucchini, rinsed and trimmed

⅓ cup extra-virgin olive oil

2 tablespoons fresh oregano or 2 teaspoons dried

¼ cup firmly packed fresh parsley leaves

2 teaspoons fresh thyme or ½ teaspoon dried

1 garlic clove, peeled

Salt and freshly ground black pepper to taste

1. Prepare a medium-hot grill according to the instructions given in Chapter 1.

2. Cut zucchini in half lengthwise. Cut a thin slice off the curved side of each half with a paring knife so that zucchini sit securely on the counter. Combine oil, oregano, parsley, thyme, garlic, salt, and pepper in a blender. Puree until smooth, and scrape mixture into a small bowl.

3. Brush both sides of zucchini halves with oil mixture and grill for 4–5 minutes per side, uncovered if using a charcoal grill, turning zucchini halves with tongs. Serve immediately or at room temperature.

Note: Both the zucchini and the oil mixture can be prepared up to 6 hours in advance and refrigerated separately, tightly covered.

4 medium ripe tomatoes

2 tablespoons extra-virgin olive oil

1 garlic clove, peeled and pressed through a garlic press

1 teaspoon dried oregano

1 teaspoon dried thyme

Salt and freshly ground black pepper

⅔ cup Greek Feta Sauce (recipe on page 20)

Herbed Tomatoes with Greek Feta Sauce

Yield: 4 servings | Active time: 10 minutes | Start to finish: 35 minutes

1. Prepare a medium-hot grill according to the instructions given in Chapter 1. Cut tomatoes in half, and squeeze gently to remove seeds.

2. Combine oil, garlic, oregano, thyme, salt, and pepper in a small bowl, and stir well. Brush mixture on both sides of tomato halves.

3. Grill tomatoes skin-side up, uncovered if using a charcoal grill, for 3–4 minutes, or until grill marks show. Turn tomatoes gently with tongs and grill for an additional 2–3 minutes, or until hot. Serve immediately, passing Greek Feta Sauce separately.

Herbed Tomatoes with Greek Feta Sauce

Sesame Radicchio

Yield: 4–6 servings | Active time: 20 minutes | Start to finish: 45 minutes

1. Prepare a medium-hot grill according to the instructions given in Chapter 1.

2. Trim root end from radicchio, and cut each head into quarters, leaving core attached. Brush radicchio and scallions with 2 tablespoons sesame oil, and sprinkle with salt and pepper. Set aside.

3. Combine vinegar, soy sauce, sherry, garlic, ginger, and pepper in a jar with a tight-fitting lid, and shake well. Add remaining sesame oil and vegetable oil, and shake well again. Set aside.

4. Grill radicchio for 3 minutes per side, covered, turning wedges with tongs. Grill scallions for a total of 4 minutes, turning them once. Remove vegetables from the grill.

5. Cut core from radicchio wedges, and cut each wedge crosswise into ½-inch strips. Cut scallions into thirds. Transfer vegetables to a mixing bowl, and toss with dressing. Sprinkle with sesame seeds, and serve immediately.

Note: The dressing can be prepared up to 1 day in advance and refrigerated, tightly covered. Allow it to reach room temperature before using.

3 (4-inch) heads radicchio

12 scallions, white parts and 1 inch of green tops, rinsed and trimmed

¼ cup Asian sesame oil,* divided

Salt and freshly ground black pepper to taste

¼ cup rice wine vinegar

2 tablespoons soy sauce

1 tablespoon mirin* or sherry

2 garlic cloves, peeled and minced

2 teaspoons grated fresh ginger

¼ cup vegetable oil

3 tablespoons sesame seeds, toasted

* Available in the Asian aisle of most supermarkets and in specialty markets.

Chapter 15

Non-Grilled Side Dishes

While there are recipes for vegetable and other side dishes in this book that are cooked on the grill, there are many times that the grill is reserved for the entree, and the supporting players are created in the kitchen. You will find those recipes in this chapter.

Setting a bountiful table with baked goods and vegetables is part of the Southern tradition. Buttermilk Biscuits and Cornbread are to the Southern states what a baguette is to France, and vegetables like collard greens and grits are also synonymous with this region.

Buttermilk Biscuits

Buttermilk Biscuits

Yield: 20 (2-inch) biscuits | Active time: 10 minutes | Start to finish: 30 minutes

1½ cups cake flour (not self-rising)

½ cup all-purpose flour

1 tablespoon baking powder

½ teaspoon salt

½ teaspoon baking soda

6 tablespoons vegetable shortening

⅔ cup buttermilk

3 tablespoons unsalted butter, melted

1. Preheat oven to 425°F, and lightly grease a baking sheet.

2. Sift cake flour, all-purpose flour, baking powder, salt, and baking soda into a large mixing bowl. Cut in the vegetable shortening using a pastry blender, two knives, or your fingertips until mixture resembles coarse meal. Add buttermilk, and stir with a fork until just combined.

3. Transfer mixture to a lightly floured surface, and knead 10 times with the heel of your hand to bring the dough together. Pat dough into a round that is ½ inch thick.

4. Cut dough into 2-inch circles and place them 1 inch apart on the prepared baking sheet. Brush tops with melted butter. Gather scraps and pat into a circle again to cut out more biscuits. Repeat until all dough is used.

5. Bake for 18–20 minutes, or until cooked through and golden brown. Serve immediately.

VARIATIONS: *For cheese biscuits, add ½ cup grated cheddar cheese to the dough. For a sweet biscuit, combine ½ cup firmly packed dark brown sugar, ½ cup finely chopped toasted pecans, and ½ teaspoon ground cinnamon in a mixing bowl, and pat mixture onto the top of unbaked biscuits.*

Note: The biscuits can be cut out up to 1 hour in advance. Do not bake them until just prior to serving.

Cornbread

Yield: 6–8 servings | Active time: 10 minutes | Start to finish: 30 minutes

1 cup yellow cornmeal

1 cup all-purpose flour

2 tablespoons granulated sugar

1½ teaspoons baking powder

½ teaspoon baking soda

¼ teaspoon salt

2 large eggs

¾ cup buttermilk

½ cup canned creamed corn

5 tablespoons unsalted butter, melted

1. Preheat the oven to 425° F. Grease a 9-inch-square pan generously.

2. Whisk together cornmeal, flour, sugar, baking powder, baking soda, and salt in a large mixing bowl. Whisk together eggs, buttermilk, creamed corn, and butter in a small bowl. Add buttermilk mixture to cornmeal mixture, and stir batter until just blended.

3. Heat the greased pan in the oven for 3 minutes, or until it is very hot. Remove the pan from the oven, and spread batter in it evenly. Bake cornbread in the middle of the oven for 15 minutes, or until top is pale golden and the sides begin to pull away from the edges of the pan.

4. Allow cornbread to cool for 5 minutes, then turn it out onto a rack. Cut into pieces, and serve hot or at room temperature.

Note: The cornbread is best eaten within a few hours of baking.

4 cups water

3 tablespoons unsalted butter

Salt and freshly ground black pepper to taste

1 cup quick-cooking grits

1½ cups grated cheddar cheese

½ cup whole milk

2 large eggs, lightly beaten

Cheese Grits

Yield: 6–8 servings | Active time: 15 minutes | Start to finish: 1¼ hours

1. Preheat the oven to 350°F, and grease an 8 x 8-inch baking pan.

2. Bring water, butter, salt, and pepper to a boil in a heavy saucepan over medium-high heat. Whisk in grits, reduce the heat to low, and cook grits for 6 minutes, or until very thick, stirring frequently.

3. Remove the pan from the heat, and stir in cheese; stir until cheese melts. Stir in milk and eggs, and scrape mixture into the prepared pan.

4. Bake grits for 45–55 minutes, or until firm in the center. Remove the pan from the oven, and allow grits to rest for 5 minutes, then serve immediately.

VARIATIONS: *Feel free to change the type of cheese; jalapeño Jack creates a spicier mixture, while a plain Monterey Jack makes the mixture creamy but not as sharp as the cheddar.*

Note: The mixture can be prepared up to 1 day in advance and refrigerated, tightly covered. If chilled, add 10 minutes to the baking time.

Cheese Grits

Scallion Hush Puppies

Scallion Hush Puppies

Yield: 6–8 servings | Active time: 30 minutes | Start to finish: 30 minutes

1. Preheat the oven to 300°F, and line a baking sheet with paper towels. Heat oil in a heavy saucepan over medium-high heat to a temperature of 360°F, or until a bread cube turns brown in 10 seconds.

2. While oil heats, whisk together cornmeal, flour, baking powder, salt, and pepper in a bowl. Whisk together egg and milk in another bowl, and then add to cornmeal mixture. Stir gently, add scallions, and stir until just combined.

3. Add batter to hot oil by 1-tablespoon amounts; this will have to be done in batches. Fry hush puppies for 2–3 minutes, turning frequently. Remove hush puppies with a slotted spoon, and drain on baking sheet. Keep hush puppies hot in the oven while frying remaining batter. Serve immediately.

5 cups vegetable oil

1 cup yellow cornmeal

½ cup all-purpose flour

2½ teaspoons baking powder

Salt and freshly ground black pepper to taste

1 large egg

¾ cup whole milk

4 scallions, white parts and 3 inches of green tops, rinsed, trimmed, and chopped

2 tablespoons olive oil

1 large onion, peeled and diced

2 garlic cloves, peeled and minced

1 green bell pepper, seeds and ribs removed, and finely diced

1 tablespoon chili powder

1 tablespoon paprika

1 teaspoon dried thyme

1 teaspoon dried oregano

1 cup tomato sauce

¼ cup water

2 (15-ounce) cans kidney beans, drained and rinsed

Salt and freshly ground black pepper to taste

Hot red pepper sauce to taste

4 cups cooked white rice, hot

Red Beans and Rice

Yield: 6–8 servings | Active time: 15 minutes | Start to finish: 35 minutes

1. Heat oil in a large skillet over medium heat. Add onion, garlic, and green pepper, and cook, stirring frequently, for 10 minutes, or until vegetables are tender. Stir in chili powder, paprika, thyme, and oregano and cook for 1 minute, stirring constantly.

2. Stir in tomato sauce, water, and beans, and simmer about 10 minutes, stirring frequently. Mash about one-quarter of beans with a potato masher, and season to taste with salt, pepper, and red pepper sauce. Serve immediately over rice.

Note: The beans can be prepared up to 2 days in advance and refrigerated, tightly covered. Reheat them over low heat, covered, or in a microwave oven.

Red Beans and Rice

Celery Seed Slaw

Yield: 6–8 servings | Active time: 20 minutes | Start to finish: 5½ hours, including 5 hours to marinate and chill

1. Combine sugar, vinegar, and oil in a small saucepan, and bring to a boil over medium heat, stirring occasionally. Reduce the heat to low and stir in celery seeds, mustard, salt, and pepper. Simmer for 2 minutes, stirring occasionally.

2. Combine cabbage, onion, green pepper, and red pepper in a large mixing bowl. Toss dressing with salad. Allow slaw to sit at room temperature for 2 hours, tossing it occasionally. Refrigerate slaw for 3–4 hours. Drain well before serving.

Note: The slaw can be made 1 day in advance and refrigerated, tightly covered with plastic wrap.

½ cup granulated sugar

½ cup cider vinegar

⅓ cup vegetable oil

1 tablespoon celery seeds

1 tablespoon dry mustard

Salt and freshly ground black pepper to taste

1 (2-pound) head green cabbage, cored and shredded

1 small red onion, peeled and thinly sliced

1 green pepper, seeds and ribs removed, and thinly sliced

1 red bell pepper, seeds and ribs removed, and thinly sliced

Sweet Potato Salad with Mustard Dressing

Yield: 6–8 servings | Active time: 20 minutes | Start to finish: 45 minutes

1. Cut potatoes into quarters lengthwise, and then into ¾-inch slices. Boil or steam potatoes for 10–15 minutes, or until tender. Transfer potatoes to a bowl and let them cool. Add onion and bell pepper to the bowl.

2. Combine vinegar, mustard, shallot, garlic, pickle relish, salt, and pepper in a jar with a tight-fitting lid, and shake well. Add oil, and shake well again. Add dressing to the mixing bowl, and toss gently. Serve at room temperature or chilled.

Note: The salad can be made up to 1 day in advance and refrigerated, tightly covered with plastic wrap.

2 pounds sweet potatoes, peeled

¼ cup finely chopped red onion

¼ cup finely chopped red bell pepper

3 tablespoons white wine vinegar

2 tablespoons Dijon mustard

1 shallot, peeled and finely chopped

2 garlic cloves, peeled and minced

2 tablespoons sweet pickle relish

Salt and freshly ground black pepper to taste

½ cup olive oil

2 pounds small redskin potatoes, scrubbed

1 cucumber, peeled

1 green bell pepper, seeds and ribs removed

1 small red onion, peeled

3 celery ribs, rinsed and trimmed

½ cup mayonnaise

3 tablespoons white wine vinegar

Salt and freshly ground black pepper to taste

Garden Potato Salad

Yield: 6–8 servings | Active time: 20 minutes | Start to finish: 4 hours, including 3 hours to chill potatoes

1. Place potatoes in a large saucepan of cold salted water. Bring potatoes to a boil over high heat, reduce the heat to medium, and boil potatoes for 10–20 minutes, or until they are tender when pierced with the tip of a paring knife. Drain potatoes and chill well. Cut potatoes into 1-inch cubes, and place them in a large mixing bowl.

2. Cut cucumber in half lengthwise and scrape out the seeds with a teaspoon. Slice cucumber into thin arcs, and add to potatoes. Cut green pepper into 1-inch sections and slice each section into thin strips. Add to the mixing bowl. Cut onion in half through the root end, and cut each half into thirds. Cut into thin slices and add to the mixing bowl. Cut each celery rib in half lengthwise and thinly slice the celery. Add to the mixing bowl.

3. Toss potato salad with mayonnaise and vinegar, and season to taste with salt and pepper. Serve well chilled.

Note: The salad can be made 1 day in advance and refrigerated, tightly covered.

6 large, very firm green tomatoes

3 cups self-rising flour

½ cup finely ground yellow cornmeal

½ cup coarse yellow cornmeal

Salt and cayenne to taste

2 large eggs

1½ cups whole milk

3–4 cups vegetable oil

Fried Green Tomatoes

Yield: 6–8 servings | Active time: 20 minutes | Start to finish: 20 minutes

1. Preheat the oven to 300°F, and line a baking sheet with paper towels. Rinse, core, and slice tomatoes into ½-inch-thick slices.

2. Combine flour, fine cornmeal, coarse cornmeal, salt, and cayenne in a shallow bowl, and whisk well. Combine eggs and milk in another shallow bowl, and whisk well.

3. Heat vegetable oil in a deep-sided skillet over medium-high heat to a temperature of 375°F; the temperature is high enough when a cube of bread browns in 15 seconds.

4. Dip tomato slices in milk mixture, and then dredge in flour mixture. Repeat once more with milk and flour mixture. Fry tomatoes for 3–4 minutes per side, turning them gently with a slotted spatula, or until tomatoes are golden brown. Drain tomato slices on paper towels, and then keep warm in the oven on the baking sheet. Repeat until all tomatoes are fried, being careful not to crowd the pan. Serve immediately.

Note: The flour mixture and milk mixture can be prepared up to 4 hours in advance. Fry the tomatoes just prior to serving.

Collards with Bacon

Yield: 6–8 servings | Active time: 15 minutes | Start to finish: 1 hour

1. Rinse collards well under cold running water. Cut off and discard ribs and thick stems, and chop remaining leaves and tender stems coarsely. Set aside.

2. Place bacon in a Dutch oven, and cook over medium-high heat, stirring occasionally, until bacon is browned. Remove bacon from the pan with a slotted spoon, and set aside. Discard all but 2 tablespoons of bacon grease. Add onions to the pan, and cook, stirring frequently, for 3 minutes, or until onions are translucent.

3. Return bacon to the pan, and add stock, vinegar, brown sugar, salt, and red pepper flakes. Bring to a boil, stirring occasionally. Add half of greens, and toss until wilted. Add remaining greens, and stir until wilted.

4. Cook greens, covered, for 45–55 minutes, or until very tender. Drain greens, and serve immediately.

Note: The greens can be prepared up to 2 days in advance and refrigerated, tightly covered. Reheat over low heat or in a microwave oven.

3 pounds collard greens

¼ pound sliced bacon, cut into ½-inch pieces

2 medium sweet onions, such as Vidalia or Bermuda, peeled and diced

1 cup chicken stock

3 tablespoons cider vinegar

2 tablespoons firmly packed dark brown sugar

½ teaspoon dried hot red pepper flakes, or to taste

Caribbean Black Bean and Papaya Salad

Yield: 6–8 servings | Active time: 20 minutes | Start to finish: 35 minutes

1. Combine beans, papaya, jicama, red pepper, and cilantro in a mixing bowl.

2. Combine garlic, shallots, cumin, cinnamon, orange juice, lime juice, vinegar, salt, and cayenne in a jar with a tight-fitting lid, and shake well. Add olive oil, and shake well again.

3. Toss salad with dressing, and refrigerate salad for at least 15 minutes before serving.

VARIATION: *Mango can be substituted for the papaya and white beans can be used instead of black beans.*

Note: The salad can be made 1 day in advance and refrigerated, tightly covered.

2 (15-ounce) cans black beans, drained and rinsed

1 ripe papaya, peeled, seeded, and cut into ½-inch dice

½ medium jicama, peeled and cut into ½-inch dice

½ red bell pepper, seeds and ribs removed, cut into ½-inch dice

¼ cup chopped fresh cilantro

3 garlic cloves, peeled and minced

3 shallots, peeled and chopped

1 teaspoon ground cumin

¼ teaspoon ground cinnamon

⅓ cup freshly squeezed orange juice

3 tablespoons freshly squeezed lime juice

3 tablespoons sherry vinegar

Salt and cayenne to taste

⅓ cup olive oil

Chapter 16

Grilled Desserts

The title of this chapter is not an oxymoron, nor is it just variations on toasted marshmallows—although it does include a recipe for S'mores. What you will find when cooking these recipes is that the grill is a natural way to glean the most luscious flavor from fruit; fruit desserts comprise the majority of these recipes. It should come as no surprise that heating enhances fruits' natural sweetness, as well as creating a softer texture.

4–6 ripe bananas, unpeeled

1 cup firmly packed light brown sugar

½ teaspoon ground cinnamon

6 tablespoons (¾ stick) unsalted butter

¼ cup banana liqueur

½ cup dark rum

1 quart vanilla ice cream

Bananas Foster

Yield: 4–6 servings | Active time: 10 minutes | Start to finish: 30 minutes

1. Prepare a medium-hot grill according to the instructions given in Chapter 1.

2. Slice unpeeled bananas in half lengthwise and crosswise so each banana is cut into quarters. Mix sugar and cinnamon, and rub mixture into cut sides of bananas.

3. Melt butter in a skillet over medium heat. Add remaining sugar mixture, banana liqueur, and rum. Cook for 5 minutes, or until hot and bubbly. Keep warm.

4. Grill bananas, covered, cut-side down for 2 minutes, or until grill marks appear. Turn bananas and grill an additional 2 –3 minutes, or until bananas are soft.

5. To serve, remove skin from bananas, and place 4 pieces in the bottom of each serving bowl. Top bananas with 2 scoops ice cream, and 3 tablespoons sauce. Serve immediately.

Note: The sauce can be prepared up to 1 day in advance and refrigerated, tightly covered. Reheat over low heat before using.

Grilled Banana Splits

Yield: 4–6 servings | Active time: 10 minutes | Start to finish: 30 minutes

1. Prepare a medium-hot grill according to the instructions given in Chapter 1.

2. Slice unpeeled bananas in half lengthwise and crosswise so each banana is cut into quarters. Mix sugar and cinnamon, and rub mixture into cut sides of bananas.

3. Grill bananas cut-side down for 2 minutes, or until grill marks appear. Turn bananas and grill an additional 2–3 minutes, or until bananas are soft.

4. To serve, remove skin from bananas, and place 4 pieces in the bottom of each serving bowl. Top bananas with 2 scoops ice cream, chocolate sauce, and 1–2 tablespoons chopped nuts. Top with whipped cream and cherries, if using. Serve immediately.

4–6 ripe bananas, unpeeled

2 tablespoons firmly packed light brown sugar

1 teaspoon ground cinnamon

8–12 small scoops vanilla ice cream

1 cup Chocolate Sauce (recipe follows), heated

½ cup coarsely chopped toasted walnuts

Sweetened whipped cream (optional)

4–6 maraschino cherries or strawberries (optional)

Grilled Banana Splits

5 ounces good-quality bittersweet chocolate

½ cup heavy cream

3 tablespoons unsweetened cocoa powder

1 tablespoon rum

¼ teaspoon pure vanilla extract

Pinch of salt

Chocolate Sauce

Yield: 1½ cups | Active time: 10 minutes | Start to finish: 15 minutes

1. Chop chocolate into pieces no larger than a lima bean, and set aside.

2. Pour cream into a 1-quart saucepan, and place over medium heat. Whisk in cocoa powder, rum, vanilla, and salt. Bring to a boil, whisking frequently, until mixture is smooth.

3. When cream begins to boil, remove pan from the heat. Add chocolate, cover pan, and allow to sit for 5 minutes; whisk well until sauce is smooth. If lumps remain, place sauce over low heat and continue to whisk until smooth.

4. Scrape mixture into a container, and refrigerate for up to 1 week or freeze for up to 3 months. To serve, microwave sauce on medium (50% power) for 30-second intervals or until liquid and warm, stirring well between microwave times.

¾ cup dark rum

8 tablespoons (1 stick) unsalted butter

¼ cup firmly packed dark brown sugar

½ teaspoon ground cinnamon

¼ teaspoon pure vanilla extract

1 ripe pineapple

3–4 cups vanilla ice cream

½ cup chopped toasted walnuts (optional)

Caribbean Rum-Glazed Pineapple

Yield: 6–8 servings | Active time: 15 minutes | Start to finish: 30 minutes

1. Prepare a medium-hot grill according to the instructions given in Chapter 1.

2. Combine rum, butter, sugar, cinnamon, and vanilla in a small saucepan. Cook over medium heat, stirring frequently, for 15 minutes, or until thickened. Set aside.

3. While sauce simmers, cut rind off pineapple, and cut in half vertically. Cut out and discard core, and cut pineapple into ⅓-inch slices. Set aside.

4. Grill pineapple slices for 1½–2 minutes per side, uncovered if using a charcoal grill, or until browned, brushing them with sauce frequently. To serve, place pineapple slices on plates and top with ice cream and additional sauce. Serve immediately, garnished with nuts, if using.

Note: The sauce can be made up to 2 days in advance and refrigerated, tightly covered. Reheat it over low heat or in a microwave oven before using.

Oranges with Raspberry Sauce

Yield: 4–6 servings | Active time: 10 minutes | Start to finish: 30 minutes

1. Prepare a medium-hot grill according to the instructions given in Chapter 1.

2. Grate 2 teaspoons zest off oranges, and then peel oranges. Cut each into 4 slices horizontally. Combine raspberries, sugar, Grand Marnier, and orange zest in a small mixing bowl. Mash fruit gently, and set aside.

3. Grill orange slices for 1½–2 minutes per side, uncovered if using a charcoal grill, or until browned. To serve, arrange orange slices on the bottom of bowls, and top with ice cream and raspberry sauce. Serve immediately.

Note: The raspberry sauce can be made up to 6 hours in advance and kept at room temperature.

- 4–6 navel oranges
- 1 pint fresh raspberries, rinsed
- 2 tablespoons granulated sugar
- 2 tablespoons Grand Marnier, triple sec, or another orange-flavored liqueur
- 1 pint vanilla ice cream or vanilla frozen yogurt

Nouvelle Peach Melba

Yield: 4–6 servings | Active time: 20 minutes | Start to finish: 30 minutes

1. Prepare a medium-hot grill according to the instructions given in Chapter 1.

2. Cut peaches in half and discard stones. Place peaches in a 9 x 13-inch pan, cut-side up.

3. Combine ⅔ cup sugar, orange juice, 1 tablespoon lemon juice, and vanilla in a small saucepan, and stir well. Bring to a boil over medium-high heat, and boil for 2 minutes, stirring occasionally. Pour syrup over peaches, and set aside.

3. Combine raspberries, remaining sugar, remaining lemon juice, and Chambord in a food processor fitted with a steel blade or in a blender. Puree until smooth, and strain mixture. Refrigerate until ready to use.

4. Drain peaches, and grill skin-side up for 4 minutes, uncovered if using a charcoal grill, then turn with tongs and grill skin-side down for an additional 3–4 minutes, or until peaches are tender. To serve, place 2 peach halves in the bottom of each bowl, and top with ice cream and raspberry sauce. Serve immediately.

Note: Raspberry sauce can be made up to 1 day in advance and refrigerated, tightly covered.

- 4–6 ripe peaches, unpeeled
- ¾ cup granulated sugar, divided
- ⅔ cup freshly squeezed orange juice
- 2 tablespoons freshly squeezed lemon juice, divided
- ¼ teaspoon pure vanilla extract
- 1 pint fresh raspberries, rinsed, or 1 (8-ounce) package frozen dry-packed raspberries, thawed
- 2 tablespoons Chambord or other berry-flavored liqueur
- 1 pint vanilla ice cream

24 sweet whole-wheat crackers, such as graham crackers or Carr's wheatmeal biscuits

1½ (3-ounce) dark chocolate bars or any flavored chocolate bar, broken into ½-inch pieces

12 large marshmallows

Ultimately Messy S'mores

Yield: 4–6 servings | Active time: 10 minutes | Start to finish: 35 minutes

1. Prepare a medium-hot grill according to the instructions given in Chapter 1. Cut 12 (8-inch) squares of aluminum foil.

2. Place 1 cracker in the center of each foil sheet, and top with chocolate. Toast marshmallows over the grill on a long-handled fork, and place on top of chocolate. Top marshmallows with remaining crackers, and enclose sandwiches in foil.

3. Grill foil packets for 2 minutes, or until chocolate is melted and gooey. Unwrap, and serve immediately.

Ultimately Messy S'mores

Candy Bar Quesadillas

Yield: 4–6 servings | Active time: 10 minutes | Start to finish: 30 minutes

1. Prepare a medium-hot grill according to the instructions given in Chapter 1.

2. Wrap tortillas in plastic wrap and microwave on high (100%) for 20 seconds, or until pliable. Spray 4 tortillas with vegetable oil spray, and place them sprayed-side down on a cookie sheet. Spread tortillas with one-quarter of cream cheese to within ½ inch of the edge. Top cheese with candy bar slices.

3. Top with remaining 4 tortillas, and press with the palm of your hand or a spatula to close them firmly. Spray tops of quesadillas with vegetable oil spray.

4. Grill quesadillas, covered, for 2 minutes. Turn gently with a wide spatula and grill for an additional 2 minutes, or until brown and crisp. Remove quesadillas from the grill, and sprinkle with confectioners' sugar. Allow quesadillas to sit for 2 minutes, then cut each into 6 sections and serve immediately.

Note: The quesadillas can be prepared 1 day in advance of grilling them. Refrigerate them, tightly covered with plastic wrap, and bring them back to room temperature before grilling.

8 (8-inch) flour tortillas

Vegetable oil spray

1 (8-ounce) package cream cheese, softened

4 (2-ounce) candy bars, such as Snickers, Almond Joy, Milky Way, or any chocolate bar, each cut into 15 thin slices

4 tablespoons confectioners' sugar

Chapter 17

Other Sweet Endings

The range and bounty of desserts in the South and Gulf Coast states reflects the varied settlement patterns, as well as the cornucopia of luscious fruits that could be harvested during the lengthy growing season. Fruits such as peaches, originally brought by the Spanish in the sixteenth century, reign supreme, and pecans are the nut of choice. Southern desserts are known for their high level of sweetness, which is luscious after a grilled meal.

2 cups pecan halves

3 large eggs

1 cup firmly packed light brown sugar

⅔ cup light corn syrup

4 tablespoons (½ stick) unsalted butter, melted

3 tablespoons bourbon

Pinch of salt

1 (9-inch) unbaked pie shell

Bourbon Pecan Pie

Yield: 6–8 servings | Active time: 15 minutes | Start to finish: 2 hours, including 45 minutes for cooling

1. Preheat the oven to 350°F. Toast 1½ cups pecans for 5–7 minutes, or until lightly browned. Chop coarsely, and set aside.

2. Combine eggs, sugar, corn syrup, butter, bourbon, and salt in a large mixing bowl, and whisk well. Stir in chopped pecans. Scrape mixture into pie shell, and arrange pecan halves on top.

3. Bake pie for 55–60 minutes, or until the center is set. Cool pie on a rack for at least 45 minutes, then serve.

Note: The pie can be baked up to 1 day in advance and kept at room temperature. Cover pie loosely with foil once cooled.

Derby Pie

Yield: 6–8 servings | Active time: 10 minutes | Start to finish: 1 hour, including time for cooling

1½ cups chopped pecans

¼ pound (1 stick) unsalted butter, melted

2 large eggs

1 cup granulated sugar

½ cup all-purpose flour

¼ cup bourbon

Pinch of salt

1 cup semisweet chocolate chips

1 (9-inch) pre-baked pie shell

Vanilla ice cream or sweetened whipped cream (optional)

1. Preheat the oven to 350°F. Place pecans on a baking sheet and bake for 5–7 minutes, or until browned. Set aside.

2. Combine butter, eggs, sugar, flour, bourbon, and salt in a mixing bowl. Beat at medium speed with an electric mixer for 2 minutes. Fold in pecans and chocolate chips, and scrape mixture into pie shell.

3. Bake pie for 30 minutes or until filling is set. Remove pie from the oven and cool on a rack for at least 20 minutes or until it reaches room temperature. Serve topped with ice cream or whipped cream, if using.

Note: The pie can be made up to 8 hours in advance and kept at room temperature. It is best eaten the day it is baked.

Lemon Chess Pie

Yield: 6–8 servings | Active time: 10 minutes | Start to finish: 3 hours, including 2 hours for cooling

6 large eggs

1⅓ cups granulated sugar

Pinch of salt

⅓ cup buttermilk

3 tablespoons yellow cornmeal

1 tablespoon grated fresh lemon zest

⅓ cup freshly squeezed lemon juice

¼ pound (1 stick) unsalted butter, melted

1 (9-inch) pre-baked pie shell

1. Preheat the oven to 325°F.

2. Combine eggs, sugar, and salt, and whisk until light and lemon-colored. Whisk in buttermilk, cornmeal, lemon zest, and lemon juice. Whisk in butter gradually, beating until smooth. Pour mixture into pie shell.

3. Bake pie for 40 minutes, or until custard is set. Cool pie on cooling rack for at least 2 hours, or until it reaches room temperature, before serving.

Note: Check the pie after 30 minutes and cover the edges with aluminum foil if they seem to be getting too brown.

1½ cups graham cracker
crumbs

⅔ granulated sugar,
divided

6 tablespoons (¾ stick)
unsalted butter, melted

1 (14-ounce) can
sweetened condensed
milk

4 large eggs, separated

⅔ cup freshly squeezed Key
lime juice

¼ teaspoon salt, divided

¼ teaspoon cream of tartar

3 tablespoons
confectioners' sugar

Key Lime Pie

Yield: 6–8 servings | Active time: 20 minutes | Start to finish: 6 hours, including 5 hours for chilling

1. Preheat the oven to 350°F.

2. Combine graham cracker crumbs, 3 tablespoons granulated sugar, and butter in a mixing bowl, and stir well. Press mixture evenly onto the bottom and up the side of a 9-inch pie plate. Bake crust for 10 minutes.

3. Combine sweetened condensed milk, egg yolks, lime juice, and pinch of salt in a mixing bowl, and whisk well. Pour into crust, and bake for 15 minutes. Remove pie from the oven, and set aside.

4. Combine egg whites, remaining salt, and cream of tartar in a mixing bowl, and beat at medium speed with an electric mixer until frothy. Increase the speed to high, and beat until soft peaks form. Slowly add sugar, and continue to beat until stiff peaks form.

5. Spread meringue on top of filling, covering it completely. Bake for 15 minutes, or until meringue is golden. Chill pie for at least 3 hours.

Note: The pie can be baked and chilled up to 1 day in advance.

Key Lime Pie

Chocolate Praline Bread Pudding with Easy Bourbon Caramel Sauce

Yield: 6–8 servings | Active time: 25 minutes | Start to finish: 1½ hours

1. For praline, grease a cookie sheet, and set aside. Combine ¾ cup sugar and water in a heavy saucepan, swirling the pan by its handle as sugar melts. Cook over medium heat without stirring for 10 minutes, until golden brown. Remove the pan from the heat, and stir in ¾ cup pecans. Immediately pour praline onto the cookie sheet. Cool completely. Chop into small pieces in a food processor fitted with a steel blade using on-and-off pulsing action.

2. For pudding, preheat oven to 350°F. Grease a 9 x 13-inch baking pan.

3. Place bread in a large mixing bowl, and set aside. Bring light cream to a boil in a medium saucepan over medium heat. Meanwhile, whisk together eggs, egg yolks, and remaining ¾ cup sugar in a medium bowl. Slowly whisk 1 cup of hot cream into egg mixture. Then, whisk hot cream-egg mixture back into cream in saucepan and cook 1–2 minutes, or until sugar dissolves. Add half of chocolate, stirring until melted. Pour mixture over bread, stirring until bread absorbs all the liquid. Stir in remaining chocolate, salt, and 1 cup praline.

4. Spoon mixture into the prepared baking dish. Place the dish in a large roasting pan with at least 1 inch of space between baking pan and roasting pan. Pour enough hot water into the roasting pan to reach halfway up sides of baking dish.

5. Bake pudding for 45 minutes, or until a knife inserted in the center comes out clean. Remove pudding from water bath and cool 10–20 minutes on a wire rack.

6. While pudding is baking, chop remaining 1 cup pecans. Combine caramel sauce, pecans, and bourbon in small saucepan. Heat, stirring occasionally, until hot. To serve, spoon sauce on top of warm bread pudding.

Note: The praline can be made up to 1 week in advance and stored in an airtight container at room temperature. The pudding can be totally baked up to 1 day in advance and refrigerated, tightly covered. Remove from refrigerator 30 minutes before serving, and reheat in a 350°F oven for 30 minutes, or until hot, covered with aluminum foil.

- 1½ cups granulated sugar, divided
- ¼ cup water
- 1¾ cups pecan halves, toasted in a 350°F oven for 5–7 minutes, or until browned, divided
- ½ pound day-old bread, cut into 1-inch cubes without crusts
- 2½ cups light cream
- 3 large whole eggs
- 3 large egg yolks
- ½ pound bittersweet chocolate, chopped
- Pinch of salt
- 1 cup caramel sauce, homemade or purchased
- ¼ cup bourbon

3 cups water

1 cup long-grain or medium-grain white rice

½ teaspoon salt

⅓ cup plus 3 tablespoons granulated sugar

½ teaspoon ground cinnamon

2 cups whole milk

1 teaspoon pure vanilla extract

3 (6-ounce) packages fresh raspberries, rinsed

2 (4-ounce) containers refrigerated vanilla pudding

Rice Pudding with Raspberries

Yield: 6–8 servings | Active time: 20 minutes | Start to finish: 3 hours, including 2 hours for cooling

1. Bring water to boil in medium saucepan over high heat. Add rice and salt, reduce the heat to medium-low, and simmer rice, uncovered, for 20 minutes, or until rice is very tender and water is absorbed. Add ⅓ cup sugar and cinnamon, and stir to blend. Add milk, and simmer for 25 minutes, stirring frequently, over low heat, or until mixture is very thick. Remove from heat, and stir in vanilla. Cool to room temperature, about 2 hours.

2. Mix raspberries with remaining 3 tablespoons sugar in a large bowl. Let stand for at least 30 minutes or until juices form.

3. Stir vanilla pudding and 2 cups fruit mixture into rice pudding. Transfer to large bowl. Top with remaining fruit, and serve immediately.

VARIATION: *This is a recipe that's open to many variations. The fruit can be chopped peaches, nectarines, or apricots as well as any combination of berries. To trim fat, 2 percent milk can be used, as can nonfat vanilla yogurt in place of the creamier pudding.*

Note: The rice pudding and berry mixture can be prepared 4 hours in advance. Cover and refrigerate separately. Bring to room temperature before continuing.

Rice Pudding with Raspberries

Warm Chocolate Tortes

Yield: 6 servings | Active time: 20 minutes | Start to finish: 35 minutes

6 tablespoons (¾ stick) unsalted butter, divided

5 ounces bittersweet chocolate, chopped, divided

2 tablespoons heavy cream

1 tablespoon rum or fruit-flavored liqueur

2 large eggs

1 large egg yolk

¼ cup granulated sugar

¼ cup all-purpose flour

Sweetened whipped cream or ice cream (optional)

1. Grease 6 muffin cups with 1 tablespoon butter. Melt 2 ounces chocolate with cream and rum in a small microwave-safe dish. Stir well and refrigerate to harden. Form chocolate into 6 balls and refrigerate until ready to use.

2. Preheat the oven to 350°F. Melt remaining chocolate with remaining butter and allow to cool.

3. Combine eggs, egg yolk, and sugar in a medium mixing bowl. Beat with an electric mixer at medium and then high speed until very thick and triple in volume. Fold cooled chocolate into eggs, and then fold in flour.

4. Divide batter among the muffin cups and push a chocolate ball into the center of each cup. Bake tortes for 10–12 minutes, or until sides are set. Remove the muffin pan from the oven and invert tortes onto a baking sheet. Move tortes to individual serving plates, and serve immediately, with whipped cream or ice cream, if using.

Note: The tortes can be prepared up to 2 hours before baking them.

Peanut Butter Mousse Pie

Yield: 6–8 servings | Active time: 25 minutes | Start to finish: 2½ hours, including 2 hours for chilling

1 cup creamy peanut butter

¾ cup granulated sugar

1 (8-ounce) package cream cheese, softened

1 tablespoon unsalted butter, melted

1 teaspoon pure vanilla extract

1¾ cups heavy cream

6 ounces bittersweet chocolate

1 (9-inch) chocolate cookie or graham cracker crumb crust

1. Beat peanut butter and sugar with an electric mixer on medium speed until light and fluffy. Add cream cheese, butter, and vanilla and beat well. In another mixing bowl, whip ¾ cup cream until medium-soft peaks form and fold it into peanut butter mixture until thoroughly combined. Refrigerate 30 minutes, or until slightly firm.

2. While mousse is chilling, chop chocolate into small pieces and place it in a mixing bowl. Bring remaining 1 cup cream to a boil over low heat in a small saucepan and pour it over chocolate. Stir until melted and thoroughly combined. Pour chocolate into pie shell, reserving about ⅓ cup at room temperature. Chill until firmly set.

3. Remove mousse from the refrigerator. Beat with an electric mixer on low speed for at least 5 minutes, preferably longer, until mousse is light and fluffy. Cover chocolate layer with the peanut butter mousse and distribute it evenly with a spatula. Place remaining chocolate in a pastry bag fitted with the small tip or in a plastic bag with small hole at one corner. Drizzle it decoratively over the mousse. Chill until ready to serve.

Note: The pie can be prepared 1 day in advance, and refrigerate, loosely covered with plastic wrap.

½ cup granulated sugar

¼ pound (1 stick) unsalted
butter, softened

2 large eggs

1½ teaspoons baking
powder

½ teaspoon pure vanilla
extract

Pinch of salt

2 cups all-purpose flour

1 cup white sesame seeds

¼ cup Asian sesame oil

Benne Wafers

Yield: 3 dozen cookies | Active time: 20 minutes | Start to finish: 1½ hours,
including 30 minutes for chilling

1. Combine sugar and butter in a mixing bowl, and beat at medium speed
with an electric mixer until light and fluffy. Add eggs, 1 at a time, beating well
between each addition and scraping the sides of the bowl as necessary. Beat in
baking powder, vanilla, and salt. Reduce the speed to low, and mix in flour.

2. Divide dough in half, form each half into a cylinder 1½ inches in diameter, and
wrap each in a sheet of waxed paper or plastic wrap. Chill rolls for 30 minutes or
until firm.

3. Preheat the oven to 350°F, and grease 2 baking sheets. Place sesame seeds in
a shallow bowl.

4. Slice rolls into ½-inch pieces. Brush tops with sesame oil, and press into bowl
of sesame seeds. Arrange cookies on baking sheets 1 inch apart. Bake for 20
minutes or until browned. Cool cookies on sheets for 2 minutes, then transfer
to cooling racks to cool completely. Once totally cooled, store in an airtight
container at room temperature.

Note: The dough can be made up to 1 day in advance.

½ pound (2 sticks) unsalted
butter, divided

3 cups all-purpose flour

⅓ cup granulated sugar

1 tablespoon cream of
tartar

2¼ teaspoons baking soda

¼ teaspoon salt

2 cups heavy cream,
divided

1 quart strawberries

⅓ cup crème de cassis or
Chambord

⅓ cup confectioners' sugar

Strawberry Shortcake

Yield: 6 servings | Active time: 15 minutes | Start to finish: 40 minutes, including
10 minutes for cooling

1. Preheat the oven to 375°F and grease 2 baking sheets with 1 tablespoon
butter. Combine flour, sugar, cream of tartar, baking soda, and salt in a medium
mixing bowl. Melt 3 tablespoons butter, and set aside. Cut remaining butter into
¼-inch cubes.

2. Cut cubed butter into flour mixture using a pastry blender, 2 knives, or your
fingertips until mixture resembles coarse meal. Add 1 cup cream, and blend
until just blended.

3. Scrape dough onto a floured surface, and knead lightly. Roll dough to a thickness of ¾ inch. Cut out 6 (4-inch) rounds and place them on the baking sheet.
Brush rounds with melted butter. Cut out 6 (2½-inch) rounds and place them on
top of larger rounds. Brush tops with butter.

4. Bake for 15–17 minutes or until shortcakes are golden brown. Cool for at least
10 minutes on a wire rack.

5. While shortcakes bake, rinse strawberries, discard green caps , and slice. Toss strawberries with crème de cassis. Set aside. Just prior to serving, whip remaining 1 cup cream with confectioners' sugar until stiff peaks form.

6. To serve, mound strawberries on larger round, and top with whipped cream and smaller round. Serve immediately.

VARIATION: *Any berry can be substituted for the strawberries, as can peeled peach slices.*

Note: The shortcakes can be baked up to 6 hours in advance and kept at room temperature.

Strawberry Shortcake

Appendix A

Metric Conversion Tables

The scientifically precise calculations needed for baking are not necessary when cooking conventionally. The tables in this appendix are designed for general cooking. If making conversions for baking, grab your calculator and compute the exact figure.

Converting Ounces to Grams

The numbers in the following table are approximate. To reach the exact amount of grams, multiply the number of ounces by 28.35.

OUNCES	GRAMS
1 ounce	30 grams
2 ounces	60 grams
3 ounces	85 grams
4 ounces	115 grams
5 ounces	140 grams
6 ounces	180 grams
7 ounces	200 grams
8 ounces	225 grams
9 ounces	250 grams
10 ounces	285 grams
11 ounces	300 grams
12 ounces	340 grams
13 ounces	370 grams
14 ounces	400 grams
15 ounces	425 grams
16 ounces	450 grams

Converting Quarts to Liters

The numbers in the following table are approximate. To reach the exact amount of liters, multiply the number of quarts by 0.95.

QUARTS	LITERS
1 cup (¼ quart)	¼ liter
1 pint (½ quart)	½ liter
1 quart	1 liter
2 quarts	2 liters
2½ quarts	2½ liters
3 quarts	2¾ liters
4 quarts	3¾ liters
5 quarts	4¾ liters
6 quarts	5½ liters
7 quarts	6½ liters
8 quarts	7½ liters

Converting Pounds to Grams and Kilograms

The numbers in the following table are approximate. To reach the exact amount of grams, multiply the number of pounds by 453.6.

POUNDS	GRAMS; KILOGRAMS
1 pound	450 grams
1½ pounds	675 grams
2 pounds	900 grams
2½ pounds	1,125 grams; 1¼ kilograms
3 pounds	1,350 grams
3½ pounds	1,500 grams; 1½ kilograms
4 pounds	1,800 grams
4½ pounds	2 kilograms
5 pounds	2¼ kilograms
5½ pounds	2½ kilograms
6 pounds	2¾ kilograms
6½ pounds	3 kilograms
7 pounds	3¼ kilograms
7½ pounds	3½ kilograms
8 pounds	3¾ kilograms

Converting Fahrenheit to Celsius

The numbers in the following table are approximate. To reach the exact temperature, subtract 32 from the Fahrenheit reading, multiply the number by 5, and then divide by 9.

DEGREES FAHRENHEIT	DEGREES CELSIUS
170°F	77°C
180°F	82°C
190°F	88°C
200°F	95°C
225°F	110°C
250°F	120°C
300°F	150°C
325°F	165°C
350°F	180°C
375°F	190°C
400°F	205°C
425°F	220°C
450°F	230°C
475°F	245°C
500°F	260°C

Converting Inches to Centimeters

The numbers in the following table are approximate. To reach the exact number of centimeters, multiply the number of inches by 2.54.

INCHES	CENTIMETERS
½ inch	1.5 centimeters
1 inch	2.5 centimeters
2 inches	5 centimeters
3 inches	8 centimeters
4 inches	10 centimeters
5 inches	13 centimeters
6 inches	15 centimeters
7 inches	18 centimeters
8 inches	20 centimeters
9 inches	23 centimeters
10 inches	25 centimeters
11 inches	28 centimeters
12 inches	30 centimeters

Appendix B

Measurement Tables

Table of Weights and Measures of Common Ingredients		
FOOD	QUANTITY	YIELD
Apples	1 pound	2½–3 cups sliced
Avocado	1 pound	1 cup mashed fruit
Bananas	1 medium	1 cup, sliced
Bell Peppers	1 pound	3–4 cups sliced
Blueberries	1 pound	3⅓ cups
Butter	¼ pound (1 stick)	8 tablespoons
Cabbage	1 pound	4 cups packed shredded
Carrots	1 pound	3 cups diced or sliced
Chocolate, morsels	12 ounces	2 cups
Chocolate, bulk	1 ounce	3 tablespoons grated
Cocoa powder	1 ounce	¼ cup
Coconut, flaked	7 ounces	2½ cups
Cream	½ pint = 1 cup	2 cups whipped
Cream cheese	8 ounces	1 cup
Flour	1 pound	4 cups
Lemons	1 medium	3 tablespoons juice
Lemons	1 medium	2 teaspoons zest
Milk	1 quart	4 cups
Molasses	12 ounces	1½ cups
Mushrooms	1 pound	5 cups sliced
Onions	1 medium	½ cup chopped
Peaches	1 pound	2 cups sliced
Peanuts	5 ounces	1 cup
Pecans	6 ounces	1½ cups
Pineapple	1 medium	3 cups diced

Potatoes	1 pound	3 cups sliced
Raisins	1 pound	3 cups
Rice	1 pound	2–2½ cups raw
Spinach	1 pound	¾ cup cooked
Squash, summer	1 pound	3½ cups sliced
Strawberries	1 pint	1½ cups sliced
Sugar, brown	1 pound	2¼ cups, packed
Sugar, confectioners'	1 pound	4 cups
Sugar, granulated	1 pound	2¼ cups
Tomatoes	1 pound	1½ cups pulp
Walnuts	4 ounces	1 cup

Table of Liquid Measurements	
Pinch	less than ⅛ teaspoon
3 teaspoons	1 tablespoon
2 tablespoons	1 ounce
8 tablespoons	½ cup
2 cups	1 pint
1 quart	2 pints
1 gallon	4 quarts

Index